The Fog Machine of War

Observations, Stories and Advice
from the Showbiz Trenches

Matt DiSero

Edited by Ariel Frailich

A Setec Astronomy Publication

THE FOG MACHINE OF WAR

ISBN 978-1-7390294-0-1

Contents

For mom and dad,
Who always thought it was possible,
even when it looked like it wasn't.

"He was his own victim, his own slave. He had made personality a profession, created a career out of selling himself. And he could not stray far, or for long, from his self-made self."

—Jim Thompson, *The Grifters*

"The ultimate sin of any performer is contempt for the audience."

—Lester Bangs

Foreword

Hi, I'm Matt Disero. I write under the name Jane Doe; it's a long story. This is a book of thoughts, ideas, quick stories and all manner of show business-related things pulled from my own writings in various formats, from published articles to social media posts. It's full of swearing, craziness, and lessons to be learned. I hope you find and use those lessons.

Two quick thoughts, then we'll begin.

Magicians all know Steve Dusheck. His effect "Wunderbar" was the first thing I saw as a kid wandering into Morrissey Magic in Toronto. I can remember with stunning accuracy the feeling of being completely blown away as that bar floated out of the test tube then over to Herb's hand. It danced up and down in a corked test tube! It was 12 dollars! I bought it immediately and was hooked for life. FOR LIFE. After that you're chasing the dragon's tail. It's perhaps the favourite of my magic memories. In all things I suppose, you never forget your first time. I knew this is what I wanted to do after I saw that. And I have. I got a lifetime of travel, memories and friends I never could have imagined, all because I walked into a magic store and a silver thing bounced up and down in a test tube. Thanks for that, Steve. One man can make a difference.

There's a scene in *Mr. Saturday Night* when Billy Crystal tells his brother what it's like on stage when you're really killing, and things are amazing: "It broke my heart you never knew what it was like when you're up there. When it's good and you're cookin'. It feels so good the laughs go right into your blood. You can be a schmuck in the afternoon but you're the king of the night, every woman wants to bang you and every man wants to know you." Horrible as it is to say, it actually IS kind of like that when you're super hot up there. It's a drug in many ways. I think it's why we all miss the approval of strangers when not onstage and try to figure out the details of how to get it when we are. Amazing how show business screwed us all up.

Someone should write a book about it.

My first time performing at the Magic Castle

"You can tell a lot about a magician by the way they hold a pack of cards."

—Herb Morrissey

June 5th 2017, 10:15 pm. I took the stage for the first time at the World Famous Magic Castle in Hollywood, California. Magic stars, greats of the industry were in the audience. Arguably some of the best working acts we have today. They're friends, but that doesn't make it less stressful. They're clearly in attendance to see if I really deserve the gig. I'll never forget that night for the rest of my life. All ego aside (if that's even possible), I think I proved booking me was not a bad decision.

If you don't know what the Magic Castle is, at its core it's the mecca for magicians, where the best in the world go to perform. It's in the middle of Hollywood, California, in the Hollywood Hills, a block up from where the Oscars awards are held. I've heard it described this way: "The Magic Castle is where lay audiences come to see great magic, and where magicians go to be great." I think that's probably true.

I have tremendous respect for the Castle and what it represents. I don't think you should be allowed to perform there unless you do. As an act, you better be in awe of that place when you walk in the door, or you just don't "get it" enough to be hired. The Castle breathes magic. Posters, ephemera, magicians everywhere, various shows; the art fills the place. It has a world-class magic library. I'm a fan of magic history and it is chock full of that, but it also ushers in the new acts in a very specific way.

I'd wanted to be a Castle act since I was young. The TV special about the Castle and its performers aired in the 90's, and after watching it I proudly proclaimed to my parents that "I will one day perform at that fine establishment," trying to sound like I knew what I was talking about. I refused to even visit to the Castle until I was hired to perform. Seriously. That was the silent deal I had with myself when I was in high school and started to perform for money. In almost three decades of performing full-time, I NEVER went to the Castle. I would honour that deal. Never go to the Castle until you're asked to perform. I will struggle towards that goal, and one day, perform there. That took nearly 30 years. Finally, it happened.

Acts from outside Hollywood aren't IN Hollywood, therefore not as easily on the radar of the people who book The Magic Castle. To that end I think it's harder for out-of-town talent to get hired. I'm based in Toronto, Canada, and trust me, it's harder to get noticed. The talent coordinator told me 3500 acts a year apply to work the stage and only about 300 get in. The competition, especially for the stage spots, is pretty epic.

When I think about all the brilliant magicians who've performed there from the 50's onward, and the regular performers who I grew up idolizing, I'm still in shock I got to play the same venue as these people. Billy McComb, Mike Caveney, Shimada, Lance Burton, Kevin James, Rudy Coby, Dai Vernon, Charlie Miller — the list is endless. I'm not saying I even approximate their level of genius, but it's pretty cool that I'm working the same place as they did. I think a lot of acts forget the history and who came before them. You should have some reverence for that. It should always be with you when you perform in that place. It SHOULD make you nervous. Who are you to be working on their stage when so many greats were at the Castle first, who likely did much better work? That should be something that reminds you to step up your game.

At the end of the day it's a thrill to perform at the best magic venue in the world. Unforgettable really. The showroom, the audiences, the atmosphere, the apartment they put me up in… all of it outstanding. Consider this. I've performed across the globe in theatres, on cruise ships, at private events and in casinos. I'm telling you the Magic Castle offers the best audiences in the world, and the best acts in the world. It's the best magic venue on the planet and it's set up in the best possible way to see great magicians work. There really is nothing like performing at the Castle. I'd heard it said for many years. It can't be explained, it can only be experienced. A thank you to the Magic Castle and the AMA doesn't even cover it.

If you're a regular performer at the magic castle I'm sure it's easy to get complacent about it and treat it like just another gig. There are twenty-one shows in a week, and the pay isn't that great. Still, it bears repeating: This is a special place where only the best get to work. You are special because you work there.

When you arrive at the Magic Castle, the doorman greets everyone. However, he says the same thing to every act, each time they walk in. It's meant to remind you that you're in the place of magic, where it lives and grows, and that it's a place particularly FOR magicians. It's where you're comfortable, special and always wanted. The doorman's greeting is simple but profound, and says what you need to hear. You walk up, he opens the door and says: "Welcome Home."

Good Night and Good Luck,
Jane Doe

Instinct

Comedians know this instinctively, I'm not sure that magicians universally do. So a friendly reminder.... In the world of bookings, talent buyers often ask how much material you have. Just came across this with a cruise contract. They ask if you have ninety minutes or two hours. Your answer might be yes, but remember that cruises and other venues will want you to break that material up. Forty-five in the theatre and then maybe two thirties in a small venue, each one a different show. So it's not standing onstage for ninety minutes or two hours. What you really need is that time WITH three openers and three closers.

There's a WORLD of difference between ninety straight and three thirties. Key to everything is the opener and the closer, the heart and brains of the show. The soft flabby middle of the act (like my own body) needs to be attended to but it's not as key the brain and heart. Hit 'em strong off the top and close strong and you're a winner every time, you just need three different ones to be successful.

Something to remember, especially as many people venture out on their first ship contracts or multiple show tours.

Good Night and Good Luck,
Jane Doe

Agents

I tagged a producer and thanked him for having used me on his show. I was shocked to find out that a number of entertainers contacted that producer after seeing my post and wanted him to start using them. I get it, it's marketing of a sort, but it sure seems kinda low rent, doesn't it? It felt like a sleazy way to approach someone who might employ you. Good producers will find YOU, don't worry about it. Then again, I've been in league with the devil for some time, so who knows what's right.

Magicians and comics can be so fucking sleazy sometimes. Nothing changes.

Agents, Speakers Bureaus, Event Planners. These are THE most important resources a corporate entertainer has. As a Toronto based, but internationally performing corporate event entertainer, here's my thinking on this topic.

I'll start off with a bad example and move on. An agent I'd heard of (with a horrific reputation) and with whom I've never done business emails this morning at not even 9 am.

"You don't know me, we've never worked together, but you'll want to. I have an offer for you, February 2019, it pays X dollars."

I reply, "The money you're offering doesn't cover the tax on my fee, also it's true, I don't know you… and not without reason." (I REALLY need a manager who can save me from myself!)

A quick note about entertainment agents and speakers bureaus. Over the course of my career I've heard plenty of entertainers tell horror stories about how much they hate agents they work for. The gripe is about the percentage they mark up. Elvis got screwed by his agent. I get it, I've had some bad ones myself. I often hear entertainers saying: "Agents make 25% to have a phone," and in the age of Google they're basically obsolete.

Don't be so sure about that. Consider this. The agent chooses YOU to pitch to their client. They have hundreds of acts to choose from, and now, thanks to Google, a WORLD of acts to choose from. They opt to profile YOU. Once you're sold to the client, agents handle everything. At least the good ones do, and it's all done for you. Venue organization, setting up and making sure the client follows your rider. Passing along the client's needs to you. Airfare, ground transportation, meals, a list of contacts and phone numbers in case anything happens along the way — oh, and they pay you. Even if the client stiffs them for money, YOU, the act, always gets paid.

You're telling me all that isn't worth a 25% markup of your fee? I often agree to a higher commission to really good planners and agents, and I'm happy to agree to whatever their markup is, IF they're good.

Case in point. My cruise agents in California are fantastic. Artists West Entertainment. Ron and Steve are the best kind of agents. Always have the backs of the performer while being sure that the client is best served by myself and my show. They deal with everything. I NEVER have to talk to the people organizing the performance. The flights, shows, all the details are given to me before I leave, packaged up in a tidy email. I literally take my ticket, show up at the airport and the machine they've organized does the rest. All I have to do is make sure when I perform I do an amazing job. I can do that every time because I can focus on the show, nothing else. When there's a problem with anything (there NEVER is, but IF there were) boom, agent help is a phone call away and one of them is always online to help or answer questions 24/7. I know this because I've used the service. They even email me every week to remind me to update my avails to make it easier for them to sell me. All that is worth commission.

The artists who complain about agent and bureau commission really need to sit back and think about what you get for that service fee. Finally, try to remember that 80% of the time or more, when a corporate, cruise or other potential client calls an agency looking for entertainment, they likely aren't requesting YOU. That agent has to decide to sell you. Be grateful they do. As an entertainer all you want to do is work on your act. Agents free up your time to do that. So put your feet up, have another latte, spin a Clash record on the turntable and write some material.

Gratitude addendum: Four hours into the flight I know it's gonna be a mess, delays at my destination. Trouble brews. Here's why you pay your entertainment agent. Artists West jumps on the phone, calls and emails the airline. You name it. New flights, everything done by the time I land in Vancouver. This on a Saturday. They continue to follow up. That's class right there. And service. And a hell of a fine agency. Respect. Add to that a hat tip to Shawn Farquhar who sees my travel post and immediately offers to help if I need gear, etc. That's how pros, friends and community work. I'm thankful. Now, I'm gonna break my foot off in this gate agent's ass. You need a good agency working with you. I've said it since the beginning. This still holds true, agents can save your ass.

As Always,
Good Night and Good Luck,
Jane Doe

Do Comedians Hate Magicians & Variety Acts?

"When you hear a crazy rumour about yourself, laugh at the insanity. Sometimes, though, rumours are very hurtful and upsetting. Not easy to brush off. That is when I urge you to please, take a deep breath, focus, take a big step back and then tell them to fuck their own face. You'll feel better."

—Me

There are lots of hacky, middle-of-the-road comedians. This is not a comparison to them, but to the original artists, the true comics. Equating comedian to variety act is difficult. If nothing else, not coming up through comedy clubs probably denies you the right to call yourself a comic. There are exceptions, but this is a look at the general state of variety.

Every comedy-oriented variety act desperately wants the title "Comedian," as if it's a loftier top tier label than variety artist or anything else. They name themselves comedian, but along with it comes a host of issues for working with genuine stand-up comics. First, there are no purely original comedy variety acts, not the same way there are comedians. I'm hard pressed to think of a magician who writes his own patter and jokes, is OF themselves then creates his or her own tricks and methods. That's what variety acts would have do to own legitimate use of the title "comedian." The undertaking would be massive; I'm not sure it's possible for a variety act to do it. However, that's what comics do. They create from the blank page all the way up to polished public ready piece of work. Again, there are variety act exceptions, but I can only think of two. I'm open to being wrong on this.

Owing to incredible luck and leveraging some friendships, I've been fortunate enough to have performed on some of the more high-profile comedy shows and comedy festivals in my country.

I don't think there's another comedy magician in Canada who's performed at as many comedy festivals, clubs and theatre tours labelled *Stand-Up Comedy* as I have. That is to say, I am a comedy magic act that does NO straight stand-up, just magic. A rarity for variety to appear and be accepted on those gigs. For the person making the referral for me getting on those shows, there's plenty of blowback. This topic often comes up. Armed with those conversations and my thirty years in show business working alongside comics, literally growing up with them, I've got something of an insight into how they see us.

So, here's what I think they see.

It's not that comics hate magicians and variety acts personally. That's a myth. Many of my close industry friends are stand-ups, I've even had intimate relationships with some. They just sort of tolerate variety acts in a working, professional environment. I think a lot of comics may even LIKE magic. It's when a variety act calls itself "comedian," or pretend that they're on the same level and want the same respect as the truly original comic, problems arise. Magicians as a group tend to be all tree, no forest. I think it's instructive to really understand that. They're not looking at the totality of their act in comparison to the comics they're working with.

Writing

Variety acts don't write. A rare few do; but 98% don't. Most variety acts are thieves, use lines from Don Alan or printed in a book from decades ago. Yet they sure don't mind calling themselves comedians. It's an issue. That 98% also do the same material, and there's little effort to find magic material others aren't doing. My cruise agent makes note on his website that if you're a magician submitting and you produce a bowling ball, make it snow, escape from a straight jacket, make a card rise from a drawing, or a table floats, don't bother to submit. I think that speaks volumes to the state of the variety. Hilariously, not too much variety in the variety world. Yet, that's still not fully the problem. A magician or juggler can work on the material at home, perfecting the piece. The magic trick can be mastered without ever stepping foot onstage.

Supposing a magician actually writes jokes; it's a good bet the joke itself hinges on the prop, situation or person they have onstage. Those are pretty easy laughs, but situational audience by-play can't be put on the printed page. You can't submit that for a TV spot. There's no script. The crutch is you can calculate the success of that by-play without having ever done it live and be pretty accurate (if only every booker knew that). The necessity to write jokes when there's someone onstage is low because of the luxury of crowd work. While that's a form of comedy, it certainly isn't stand-up comedy writing per se. It's a massive conundrum I have with my own show. Comedy bookers will tell you that if you're doing crowd work, they probably won't look at you. Very few comics have mastered that skill. VERY few. Mike Bullard, a Canadian comedian, IS a master at it. No one better in the country, but he can't get TV shows like *Just for Laughs* or *Winnipeg Comedy Festival* because he can't write a script. Nothing to submit for censors to clear for air. They can't trust he'll be clean. That's an issue for variety too. It's also something comics frown upon. If it's not on the paper it's in the vapour.

Contrast to the comic who cannot work out the joke unless they're in front of real people. You HAVE to go out every night and work it live. You can write it at home, after a long while in the business you get a sense of how or IF that joke might work, but not until that comic is in front of an audience do they really know. Stand-up requires direct feedback from an audience to see the true success of a piece. I'm not sure that rings true for variety. If you juggle 6 balls or make a duck appear, there WILL be applause. If you have jokes about a juggler having big balls and the animal being "ducking" impossible to appear, those jokes aren't any good, easy, and come with the prop. They'll also get a laugh of some kind, I guarantee that. A lot of magicians think that's enough, and they think that's something to be proud of. Comics think otherwise. They think it's too easy. They're correct.

The real issue is craft

A comic I worked with on a theatre tour said it best: "Massaging the jokes in a set is like being Andy Dufranse in *Shawshank Redemption.* You're in the yard, slowly polishing the chess pieces of your act. One bit at a time, over years. Literally years of sets. Until finally all the bits come together and you can start playing the game." Variety acts get the luxury of being able to carve out and smooth that piece quickly, often within weeks and start playing immediately. Many of the jokes have been written and tried out by someone else in the past so getting them to work for you isn't that difficult. It's true, variety acts have to keep working material out, but it's a massive head start. If a magician finds a wrinkle in an old joke and uses it, that's considered fine. If a comic does that, it's considered hack.

Style

Comics have no choice but to paint a picture the whole audience sees in unison or the joke doesn't work. It's much easier to paint that picture when there are props and the show is in the moment. Nothing for the audience to relate to. For a comedian's material to work, the point of view must come from a place everyone understands at once. Those two things are vastly easier for variety acts. I don't think comics see that advantage as fair. Additionally, the nature of variety is wildly different than straight stand-up. It changes the rhythm of a show and makes it impossible to follow with monolog stand-up. Comics don't like following that variety energy.

To combat this, savvy bookers put the magic act at the end of the show. The headline position. It's yet another problem. No comedian gets to rocket to headliner slot, but because of props in the set, variety does. It's not uncommon for a stand-up to work 6 or 10 years, maybe more, to become a headliner, carving out 45-60 min of material. If that's you, imagine one night working with an act who's bought their tricks and stolen old jokes. Now that act gets to be headliner and get the highest pay. I'm sure you can see where the problem sits.

Patton Oswald has a bit about working with a magician that demonstrates this. Yes, I know who that unnamed magician is....

The reality

I ask myself every time I work a comedy festival or club or multi-comic theatrical tour, "Am I justly taking a spot away from a harder working, more dedicated comedian? Do I deserve the same respect as these people? Do I get title 'comedian'? Should I get a spot over a comic who's spent years finessing each word, editing, distilling, making each joke stronger? Should I get that spot over them?" The answer is... I shouldn't. Tough pill to swallow, but it's true. Thank God showbiz isn't a meritocracy. I don't get to own the title 'comedian'. I wonder if you think you do? Does your act deserve that label? I've worked my act in various forms for almost three decades and I continue to write material. Sometimes by myself, others with the help of comics. No matter how many comedy festivals I work, I can't say what I do stand-up comedy in the truest sense. If I were one of those acts that did, I think that's where the divide between act relationships begins. A friend and comedian of some fame always says that while I am not a comedian, I am "in the fraternity of comedians." Maybe that's the very best we can hope for as variety acts.

Thoughts for the writers room.
Good Night and Good Luck,
Jane Doe

Regrets in Show Business

> *"Always dreamed if show business crapped out on me and I had to get a 'job,' I'd take my prop case of stuff and throw it into the depths of Lake Ontario, never to be seen again. I realize I have a Pelican case. They float. Show business fucked me again."*
>
> —*Me*

"You follow them out of the clubs, or they follow you out of the clubs." I've heard that since I was 16 or 17 years old when I was starting out in comedy clubs. I totally ignored it. To this day my greatest regret in my show business career is that I never built a fan base. Chasing them out of the clubs was a mistake. I should have been figuring out a way to get them to follow me. Had I been smart about it, I'd have a following who would come to see me throughout their lives. Instead I chose to go after money and gigs and travel. It was a giant mistake. Most of my working career has been corporate after-dinner events like conferences and conventions. Cruise ships also, and occasionally in theatre shows with other acts. The money and travel have been wonderful. No question. That's where I've performed the most once I left the world of comedy clubs. The money generated from those things has been substantial. The front end of my career was pretty great. In August it'll be the anniversary in this business but I'll forever have to be chasing gigs. That was something I did not see coming. The non-stop, relentless hustle and being at the mercy of someone else. It's preferable to end your career with people coming to you.

Contrast that to this imaginary scenario. Had I built an audience while I was in comedy clubs, those people would have kept coming to see ME. Then I could have demanded more money in clubs, kept building and moved on to smaller and then bigger theatres. They'd have come to see me every year because they'd be genuinely interested in my work and what I'm doing new. I would control when and how I work. Not a corporate planner or cruise ship who may or may not even want me. The nature of your material is also dictated by the environment in which you perform. My current act is streamlined to play perfectly to the conference and convention crowds and the more mature audiences of higher-end cruise ships. I particularly kill on Holland America Line. Perhaps on Carnival Cruises full of younger people, I may not fare as well. I wonder what interesting artistic choices I may have made had I just stayed poor a little longer. Should have kept working clubs where people could see me. Then, invested into building that fan base and material they like and relate to. I'll never know. That's the moral of this story: Don't make the same mistakes I did. Chasing money isn't what you got into this for. If money was something you wanted, you'd be able to make it in some other industry quicker and more plentifully. Keep reaching out to audiences, it's cool to be poor for a while longer. Keep building that email list and be genuine with your audience. They'll come to see you. When that happens, you're never beholden to anyone, and your work life is truly your own.

Wishing you all the success.
Good Night and Good Luck,
Jane Doe

Rando Thoughts

"Memes are the cave paintings of today," is what I wrote in my notebook while on my way to meet a friend the other day. Didn't know what I'd do with it, but thought it would be useful to frame something down the road. Turns out that line turned into this whole new cool thing. Point is, no matter what line or bit of business pops into your head, ya better write it down, never know where it'll lead. Write it down, because it'll never come back if you don't. If it ain't on the paper, it's in the vapour.

Reminder for the day.
Good Night and Good Luck,
Jane Doe

The Sound of Silence

Corporate events, from an entertainment perspective, work like this: they'll be a good crowd if there's table chatter. Lots of talking and laughing during the meal indicates a nice, happy crowd. Quiet with no talking means it'll be a tougher crowd, one you need to work harder to win. Knowing this helps you plan your attack. It's all about the first two minutes. That's what makes you sink or swim. It's part of the physics of how this job works.

My crowd tonight is largely Amish. A lot of bonnets here, and they're silent. Not a peep out of the lot of em. Imma sink like a stone.

Oh. There's no booze here, so I can't even have a happy send off.

Thoughts from the Ministry of Planning and Development.
Good Night and Good Luck,
Jane Doe

Magicians

> *"Magicians are creatures of habit. There's something comforting in the consistency, you know it'll happen. Local magicians come to the show, hang out after for meet and greet and you know 10 of you will end up at some bar with beer and packs of cards talking moves and effects."*

> *"I read in the Zarrow book rolling your little finger at such and such a point makes this thing work better"... the passing of knowledge... it's the kind of thing a fly on the wall would hear. I don't deny that it's sad and nerdy, but it's social. All these years later, I still secretly kinda love it.*

This is a story but it's worth it, I think....

I miss Willis Kenny, he was a great magician and a real character. Say what you will, we don't have enough crazy characters like that dude anymore. Thanks to Charles McBurney I got to spend tonight watching videos of Willis doing magic and it was great. REALLY great! I felt like a kid again at the magic club. I never thought I'd get to hear his raspy, boozy voice again.

I first met Willis Kenny in my mid or late teens, we were both members at the magic club in Toronto. He had baller status then because he was a mentor of Gary Kurtz and I'd heard he'd hung with Vernon, even fooled him a few times. His card work was, to the very end, exemplary. Cups and balls were killer. Any way you slice it, you'd want to see him do something at the club. But... he sure wasn't the warmest guy to new kids. No secret he was a bit of a problem drinker, so... whatcha gonna do. Hey, I was drinkin' then as well. Heather Spindler vanished on me like a fart in the wind and I figured it was a good time to drink that puzzle away. So we had that in common.

At the time when you joined the magic club you had to perform for the members or you couldn't get in. I no longer believe that to be the case. It was like Fight Club. First time there, you HAVE to fight. Believe me when I tell you, old crabby magicians watching you or shirtless, bare-fisted fighting, to this day I'd choose the fight. As a kid it's nerve-wracking doing magic for other magicians. They aren't the best audience, judgemental, and sure aren't laughers. Point is, I decided to do whatever Jay Sankey trick was in vogue at the time, I think something with a pay envelope and a hole punch (some things never change) — a good, strong, quick effect. Nervous but got through it, I was proud of that. Willis chewed me out about that trick. "Too much for you, that trick, put an apple on your head and give some guy the gun and let him shoot… grumble… grumble." I dunno WTF he said or meant, I think he preferred the classics. Anyway, over the years he warmed to me. I really did enjoy spending what limited time I got with him. I learned a fair bit along the way too, just by watching. There's the thing: I really wish I'd worked harder to spend more time with him. I never knew him like Charlie did, but it was nice to see him holding court at the club or at the bar every so often. I should have hung out after the lectures more. I should have made more of an effort to show him things I was working on. I wonder what else I might have learned but never did. If I just had the stones to show him more…. I guess I'm saying it's important not to ignore the older people. When they're gone… they're gone and you aren't gonna have access to them any more. Getting these videos of Willis was a real treat. I got lucky. There's one of him in a convention hotel room, drink next to him, it's so much fun. You might not get so lucky with video as I just did today. So make sure you hang out with the old guard now and again. Even if they're grumpy. It's wise to be mindful to keep up with people older than you. You'll learn something. Healthy for both of you. I'm gonna pour one out for Willis now.

Good Night and Good Luck,
Jane Doe

Unsolicited Advice for Performing on *Penn and Teller: Fool Us*

If you just got cast for Fool Us, CONGRATULATIONS!

You're about to appear on easily the best television program that showcases magic since *The Paul Daniels Magic Show*. You will perform on the nicest stage I've ever worked in my career performing across the globe. You just won the lotto. Seriously. Penn and Teller treat you like an equal and give you every shot at killing. It's the best. That said, you're undoubtedly nervous about the experience and what's about to happen to you. It's also general advice worth considering.

You may not have thought of this, but I wish I knew these things before I went to tape my own spot in Season 3. So, here it is.

First, EVERYONE on that production wants you to kill. EVERYONE. it's not about fooling P&T, it's about you having an amazing set and making great television. They're not even secret about it, fooling them is NOT a priority. They just want great magic from you. Seriously, everyone is in your corner.

LISTEN and heed the advice of Michael Close and Johnny Thompson (edit: Johnny has sadly passed away, and at the time of this edit, it's only Micheal Close working as production), the magic consultants on the show. Mike has 40 years experience in magic and many years experience shooting the fastest-paced production I've ever been a part of, and he's a hell of a nice guy who's crazy funny. I promise he knows what he's talking about. Johnny Thompson is the master, if he says do something, make that adjustment. You couldn't afford these two guys to consult on your show unless you're wealthy, but guess what… it's here, for free! Listen to them. it's hard to swallow, but do it. Listen to the producers who have infinitely more experience than you regarding what makes TV look good. No one is trying to take you down a peg by making suggestions. These people seriously are the nuts and bolts of this production and believe me when I tell you, they can see things about how your set looks on TV that you cannot. Everything they offer is there to help you. I pushed back on some things I wish I hadn't. It was a waste of time.

In my first tech rehearsal Johnny Thompson fell asleep. That was a kick in the balls. OK, he was REALLY sick that day, really sick, and it was second to last day of filming, and Johnny's what, 70?…. The guy was wiped out, but… it hurt. Still, production offered some changes to my set and he did manage to stay awake to watch my spot, afterwards he gave me a piece of advice that I use EVERY single live show I perform and it makes that hunk WAY better. You honestly can't put a price tag on this advice. IF you could hire these guys it would cost thousands of dollars for that advice. You're getting paid to have these people bump up your act. What a gift. Take it in. Trust me.

Regarding the actual shoot. Look, I've been a full time act since I was 16. I've never had a day job. I'm a lifer and as a result, like many of you, the social aspect of being on a multi-person show is huge. It IS the juice. I have better sets when I'm joking around with the other acts before I go on. It helps me get into the zone. This will NOT happen on Fool Us. When you shoot you'll be isolated from the other acts.

You can't watch them do camera block, tech rehearsal or shoot the live show. You can't be in the audience. You literally sit in a little room waiting to be called to go out and tape. After makeup you're kind of in a jail cell. If you're hoping to hang with the acts backstage, forget it. Afterwards in the bar, yes, but during the show, no. It's hard to be alone and not get to chill with the acts, especially on such a high-pressure shoot. Be aware of that and get ready for it. It's a mind screw if you're used to production shows where socializing is a big part of it. Just an FYI, find a way to get into your own head space without other acts around or it'll hurt your set.

For many of us, Penn and Teller were people we admired growing up. I loved their short films, movie and TV appearances. If you're of a certain age, it WILL head fake you to walk out and see your heroes sitting 20 feet from you. Just remember, work your act. You're a pro, work the material. Ignore them for those 7 minutes. Don't get hung up on what they think of you. I really wish I had done that.

End of the day, as my friend Glenn Ottaway rightly points out, they're using you and you're using them. They use you for material to fill their show, you use them for profile and the tape. That's the exchange. It doesn't matter what they think of you in the moment. It makes for good TV for them to be seen liking your work, so don't think they're being super judgmental. Just do the material you've worked for all these years. You'll be great. If a joke doesn't fly, don't worry. If the audience doesn't get it, the laugh track will (old TV joke, but kind of true).

That little advice brings me to the show itself. Remember, this is a 2-week shoot. Two shows a day for 14 days, plus the crew shoots Penn & Teller segments within that time too. it's exhausting for these people. My advice to you is to try and get on early in the shoot and early in the show. Early in the shoot (days 1-5 or 6) you get a fresher crew and a fresher P&T.

Key, it seems to me, is to get on early in the actual show. 1st or 2nd position is ideal. Comedy club thinking is 3rd spot is the best for a showcase. This is not that. Unlike every other comedy production show I've done live or on television, with *Fool Us* there's a gap between each act as they strike the stage and reset. I followed a dude with a zillion props left on the stage. The host intro'ed him. He went on first with his 7 minutes, then there was 30 minutes of strike and reset, then the host again, then I went out. The audience saw two acts do 7 minutes each in about 45 min. If you don't think that down time drains the crowd, you shouldn't be on the show. BE READY FOR THAT.

Vegas is a travel town, If you tape on a traditional travel day like a Friday, the audience won't be as hot as they might be on a Saturday night. Get ready to come out swinging. Always swing for the fences. There's a warm-up comic for in-between acts as production resets, but it doesn't seem to help. I advocate for doing material that you open with, not close, because it's naturally stronger material from the beginning of your show and doesn't require the full length of your normal show for the audience to like you and doesn't have the build that your closing piece might depend on. it's natural to assume you'd want to use your closer for the TV show (I did) but it's best to use a punchy opening piece that establishes likability and strong magic.

Let me leave you on this, what I think is the most important thing. There's a rule in comedy clubs — which is where I came up in show business — and that is: Don't be a stage hog. In other words, don't go long, amongst other things. The same sort of thing applies here. Seriously, DO NOT be a douchebag and fight with Penn and Teller. This show is about making magic look amazing, giving you a great tape that you could never in a million years afford to make yourself and having a fun spot. Fooling Penn and Teller should be so low on your list of priorities that it's not even noticeable. Listen to me closely here, if you fight with them about method or some B.S. little bit of something in an effort to say you fooled them… you accomplish nothing. NOTHING !!

The big win for the show is BEING ON THE SHOW. You already got that. No one ever got more gigs because they fooled P&T (unless you sell magic to magicians). It's best to go on and look like a boss and thank them for the wonderful opportunity of being on the show. They just gave you the best gift of your whole career. I wish I could personally thank Teller and Penn. They seriously helped my career more than anything else thus far. You will get international work out of this show. Why be a Dbag? Do not fight with them, do not nitpick with them, be honest, let them have the win even if it's kind of unclear. If Penn says the name of the trick you did, isn't that enough? He doesn't need to go into detail about the method. Let it go. It is, after all, their show. Unless you honestly freaked them out, let it go.

This accomplishes two things.

1) It makes you look like a pro and not petty. Additionally, that arguing you'll do will most likely be cut out in editing, so really, why? You only piss them off.

2) This is key. PLEASE remember, someone has to follow you on that show. I had to follow a guy that argued with P&T so much (and remember, you have zero idea what's going on with the taping prior to you walking out, so you have no idea what the act ahead of you has done) that, when the P.A. walked me out to my mark to start my shoot, I looked across at Penn and could tell he was visibly pissed off. You know how hard it is to focus on your set or anything else when you see your hero pissed and you wonder what the hell you think YOU did to do this to him? I had friends in the audience for my taping and they said Penn was indeed pissed with this guy. Bad when the audience notices. So bloody unprofessional of that act. I'd love to name him, but I won't. To Penn's credit, he treated me with respect and he was fun and funny with me and gave me a really useable pull quote (another bonus of being on the show). I owe him for that. He's a celebrity and didn't have to check himself for my benefit, but did. He could have gone any other way.

So… be a pro and be nice to them, and in return they'll be nice to you. It helps everyone, including the act that has to follow you. Keep your ego in check. You're on the show. You've got the brass ring, don't let it slip away by being petty about fooling them. Trust me, even if you fool them, your cock remains the same size. Let it go.

Oh finally, for the love of God, treat the crew kindly. I shouldn't even have to tell you this if you're a pro, but I've heard stories… so, remember the actual people who make you look and sound good are the crew, not you, not Penn and Teller, not Close or Thompson. Be nice to the the crew !!! — lest your mic cut out or your makeup look like crap or you're lit weirdly. Be a proper human being to these working pros. It's to your benefit and guess what, it's the human thing to do anyway.

Good Night and Good Luck,
Jane Doe

Some Things Never Change

Gig inquiry comes back $2400 cheaper than I quoted. I write back: "You're the same person that shows up to the strip club with a handful of coupons, aren't you?" This business savvy is why I've always been better off having an agent represent me.

While performing at the Magic Castle, I was invited to Mike Caveney's house with two friends for an afternoon. At the time I was feeling particularly beaten down by the business. The constant hustle, risks (both financial and emotional) and a general sort of malaise about where the hell this was all going.

Mike is known for his extraordinary poster collection, but he also has a tremendous collection of correspondence from magicians dating back to the early 1900's. While my friends were trying to broker a poster sale with Mike, I asked permission to read through some of the collections of letters between acts he'd bound into books. They're hidden in a pretty cool place in the house and there's a ton of them. Perusing the letters acts wrote to each other more than 100 years back, I was shocked, amazed and pleasantly surprised to find that they all had EXACTLY the same gripes I do now. Four-walling a theatre and the financial risks, the promotion of it all, will there be enough asses in the seats, competition, are there gigs enough, travel BS, etc. It was, in a way, reassuring that some things never change. It really buoyed my spirits.

For a time, I'd considered cashing in my chips on the business, but that experience really changed my mind. It's likely we all forget that people have the same issues in any business, but artists just don't talk about it as much amongst each other. I don't know Mike that well, don't even think he's on Facebook, but I ought to write him a letter of thanks. Reflecting on that experience this morning I realized that in all of our technological email awesomeness, I bet what's going to be lost for future generations is the correspondence between acts.

The letters performers would write to each other on the road by way of physical mail, and therefore leaving behind a permanent record of their thoughts, has vanished now into the ether of text messages and emails that are likely never saved and curated. A lot of books and videos are produced of late, and that's wonderful, but the nuts and bolts of the business is always passed on act to act. Elbow knowledge, as the trades would say. The real work of things is rarely published. In the last decade at least all the really great bits of business have come from other acts in the form of broken up texts, and emails. I wonder if all this electronical, ease-of-use, instant-gratification stuff is leaving behind a dark ages of magic that will only be revealed 100 years from now as acts look to learn from whatever we're doing now, only to find hard drives wiped out by a giant magnet. Or, maybe I'm old school and I can't see it. It's probably that, right? What do I know? I still type thank you cards to clients on an Underwood typewriter.

Food for thought,
Good Night and Good Luck,
Jane Doe

Tech for Corporate Events

Ever get on the phone with a potential client who's taking a poop? Like, right there, in real time? I just got off the phone with one.... I straight up said "Are you for real, taking a dump right now? WTF happened to business? I can't even believe it... I heard the splash and everything." I probably won't get that gig. I could use the money, but someone's gotta stop this poop calling. Thank God there's no smell phones, but I bet they're coming.

Edit: He just called back and is STILL doing it. Someone's playing Jumanji or something.

Forty years ago today Sony released the Walkman. It changed music and the way we interact with the world; or, more to the point: how we *don't* interact with it. Nothing was going to be the same after that first Walkman came out; a game-changer. Then Apple came along and changed the game again. As I'm sure something will come to make the iPhone / iPod era look quaint and old-fashioned. Brings me to an interesting point about entertainers, comedy acts especially. Many of them eschew tech in their shows, instead opting for the basic general wash of white light on the stage and a microphone on a stand. I'm one of those people. I have no tech in my show. I want the audience to focus on me and what I'm saying, and it has to be ME that creates the show... BUT... I think it's unwise to hire talent that has zero use or access to technology to add to their performance. While it's true I don't use any tech onstage, I have remote control music and screen images for pre-show, as people walk into the venue and are seated and settled. For cruise ships that I perform on such as Holland America, who have discerning audiences who are used to seeing theatre, this is very important. That sets a tone, and that's important. Images on the screen say something about the show they're going to see and about who I am. All that before I've even walked onstage. There's pre-show video to give the audience a chance to sample what they're about to see. It keeps them occupied for the otherwise boring transition from seating until performance time. It keeps them up and laughing. It also keeps the crowd at an energy level that's easy for me to work with. That gets done in pre-show and it's time I don't have to use onstage to build up the audience. I'm more impactful right away. Always a better place to be. I use technology for everything that surrounds my show in the hopes of building profile, anticipation and setting mood. These things can all be leveraged to increase the impact of the show. That's what I want. Everyone to have an amazing time. Too many entertainers don't give any consideration to pre-show tech and let it slide.

Just my two cents for things to think about.

Until next time,
Good Night and Good Luck,
Jane Doe

Standing Ovations

> *"8 weeks away, 12 countries, flights, hotels, crap ton of shows and one Demi Moore in St Elmo's Fire-type breakdown later, I'm finally... HOME!"*

Here's the thing. I LOVE performing on ships. The theatres and tech crews are amazing, and they treat headline entertainers like me really well. It's a joy and an honour to perform on their vessels. In the last 8 weeks I've performed on five ship stages. From the newest ship in the world, The Nieuw Statendam to the oldest and most character filled in the fleet, the Rotterdam. Every single show was fantastic. Each one, without exception. I ended my run of shows with a rousing standing ovation.

Comedy is an interesting beast. I've often heard it said that they (the audience) don't "stand" for stand-up. It's true. For some reason audiences don't see comedy as something they should stand up and applaud for every time they see it performed really well. Music or production-type shows get it easier and people stand almost out of habit at the end of those, even if they're not great. I have the fortunate advantage of magic in combination with stand-up and have an interactive edge to the show that allows me to pull a standing ovation more often than a straight stand-up comic. There's nothing terribly important about getting the standing ovation. In fact as crowds become younger and less used to seeing entertainment in a theatrical setting, the less they give encores or standing O's any thought, no matter how much they loved the performance. They simply don't know what an ovation is, or that there's etiquette to performances. That said, I do enjoy getting those elusive standing ovations. It's an old school seal of approval for myself. It makes me feel like I'm doing my job. Conversely, performances where I have not received the coveted standing O are often the best in the minds of the passengers who see the performance. Proof of that are the ratings and comments I hear around the ship. End of the day, what I'm saying is this: The standing O can no longer be used as a metric for the success or quality of a comedy based act, BUT, when they come around it's really nice. If I see one more act use flags or a story about promising their kid a standing O to make them feel better, or some other awful hack to get the audience to stand, I'm gonna punch that act right in the baby maker.

Until then, don't forget to stand and applaud a fine performance....
Good Night and Good Luck,
Jane Doe

Growth

Hotels across America have vending machines and potted plants. Behind those machines and in the foliage of the plants, comedians have hidden a joint for "when they come back." I miss trying to find those treasures, it was a good hobby.

At a comedy club / hotel in upstate New York, behind a coke machine, I found one so yellowed and brittle I swear it must have been from 1985.

Man, I miss the road.

Most of the work I've done around the world in my career as a magician and comedian is corporate in nature. Conferences, conventions, retreats. Anywhere a company or group of companies has a meal, I can be entertaining after that meal. It's been a remarkable journey. A product of my environment, I've tried to create a show that's hassle-free. It helps both me and the client. It's kept me working. A comedy magic show that can be performed in the round and works for groups of 10 to 5000. The biggest crowd I've performed for was at Calgary's Saddledome. 8000 people. I'm a monologist at heart, just happens there's magic and audience interaction throughout the act. Frankly it's THE winning combination for a bulletproof, corporate entertainment package. Interestingly, in the last few years I've been performing at more and more theatres. Same show with little tech. General stage wash and a microphone. It's a strong show. I work damn hard for that. However, the artist in me would like to incorporate music and lighting into the show when I'm working these theatrical venues. It's not like I've never thought about it before. My notebooks are filled with scads of ideas for music and other production elements to the show. I've never really got to implement them because, for a corporate event, I never want to be the problem child of stage tech. I'd much rather go in, do an amazing job and not be too much of a bother to anyone. The MacGyver of comedy magic. For theatrical work, I'm paying for techs to be there anyway, so I may as well use them and their services. It's good to grow a bit creatively. I never want to be the act that looks and sounds the same now as I did 20 years ago. I'm currently working on a new closing piece for my show that I'd originally written as a monologue, but now I'm working on laying down music as a background track and using a lighting effect to make the piece pop. It's been a joy tracking down music that works, and as a film score junkie, tremendous fun barely covers the thrill of this. Of course, I'll workshop the piece both ways, with tech and without, so that I can maximize its utility for both corporate and theatrical work. I'll always remember that corporate work supports my family and I'll always be mindful of making that show work. Still, theatres are there to work, so grow or die, baby.... Grow or die. Wait, I probably won't use the tech after all, but you should try it.

See ya at the sound board....
Good Night and Good Luck,
Jane Doe

Opportunities

"The dildo of consequences rarely arrives lubed.

Tonight I'm supposed to be performing at this corporate event in a mansion. They changed the location to, get ready for it, an open-air patio at some restaurant where no one will be seated and the chaos of the venue will run in the background as I'm trying to work. They don't even understand why it doesn't work if people are standing, let alone the other logistical issues.

I'm often asked why we charge such ungodly amounts of money for corporate events. Why celebrity comics and performers loathe corporate. In part we charge for experience, the show's profile, and knowing how to kill for that demographic with consistency. Mostly though, We charge a lot because of the bullshit factor that's always at play.

Truth is, the ones that hire entertainment without knowing anything about why it works and where, are the same ones that bitch the most when the garbage they hand you makes it not work.

Trash for cash tonight baby... that's how it is."

—Me

You need someone to believe in you just enough to get you started. "You need to get your break," you hear that in show business. Or, "I never got my break," you hear that a lot too, probably more often. Here's the thing: Almost every great experience I've had in my show business career has come from friends in the industry. Those relationships are the real break. If you're fortunate you'll work with nice, genuine people who will help along the way. I'm super lucky. Any time I've been booked on something I've wanted like TV, a comedy festival, or a venue I've wanted to play it's always a friend who's helped set that in motion. You never know where the help is going to come from.

Pro tip: It's a good idea to be ready when the opportunity hits, so never stop working hard, but you almost always need someone to help you get there.

Recently I was honoured to be asked for some writing help by an extremely talented comedian. An exceptional writer and experienced performer with more television exposure than I'll ever have, including several *Tonight Show* spots, many with Johnny Carson. He'd asked for help with writing a radio set that he was doing in a month's time. This is EXTREMELY rare. Stand-up comics, especially of that stature, don't need help writing and never want help from a variety act. I'm well aware he wasn't asking because I'm a great writer, he's got access to hundreds of the best comics in the country he could go to for help with jokes. He came to me because the topic of material is in my particular wheelhouse. Something I know about. Maybe he just wanted to see what I could do with it. Just to see if the rumours were true that variety acts can't write. Either way, he didn't need the help. The fact remains I DID help write the piece. Out of this experience I got something FAR more valuable than money. I got to see the way one of the world's foremost comedians structures their work. The process. You can't pay for access to that kind of information. Free, on-the-job training, and after almost 30 years in show business I'm pleased to report I learned some stuff that had escaped me before.

I offer a joke or an avenue to explore, and he says yes or no and then why, where and how it should be inserted into the set. Or, why the joke is useless. Most striking to me was that when I thought we were done we did a final read through of the piece. It had been read aloud many times, and I believed it to be quite good, then a week later he calls and reads it to me again. The same jokes and material are there, but small changes make it perfect. It was an education to see how to manipulate a turn of phrase, a word here or there or changing tone of delivery augments the piece for the better. I know all this stuff, and how to apply it, but the sheer speed at which he applied it was fascinating. The great acts can polish sets like that. There's the difference between them and everyone else. That, and the ability to instantly spot a working joke and shape many of them into something coherent and funny.

End of the day, I got to do this. That's the luck people talk about in show business. I still had to be able to deliver, but getting the opportunity to do so... that's the break. I wouldn't have otherwise had the chance to work with another comic on something like this, it's just not something variety acts get to do. Now I can take this opportunity and apply the lessons learned from it to my own writing and also use it as leverage to perhaps work the same radio show. This is the nature of relationships in show business. It's also proof that at end of the day you should be nice to everyone, always, in all walks of life. It's the right thing to do and you never know where it's going to lead. Just be ready for when something comes along. In this case, I got the confidence to know I'm good enough to write with other talent.

Until next time,
Good Night and Good Luck,
Jane Doe

Risky Business

I'd always heard that James Brown was a legendary asshole. I can't confirm, but the rumour persists. I just heard the best story about him. It's so show business. Finished the concert, and goes to the dressing room. The crowd is cheering for an encore. Promoter goes to his dressing room and it's locked. Bangs on the door. "James, they want an encore." Brown replies, "Keep sliding money under the door, I'll come out when it's enough."

To quote the movie *Risky Business*, "Sometimes you gotta say, 'What the Fuck,' make your move. Joel, every now and then, saying 'What the Fuck,' brings freedom. Freedom brings opportunity, opportunity makes your future."

Miles, played by Curtis Armstrong, was right. I've largely based my career on this one simple thought. I just spent 11 days on this ship The MS Rotterdam. What a fantastic time. Halifax, Bar Harbour, Boston, an OVERNIGHT in Manhattan, Charleston, Key West, Tampa, then home to Toronto. I went to Cheers in Boston because… you have to. As Norm says, "It's a dog-eat-dog world and I have Milk Bone Underwear." As cruise ship runs go, that's a brilliant itinerary. I couldn't have been happier. What a great gig. If you're ever on it, hit the custom stone oven pizza place on the back of deck 9. WOW… buckle up. So, to my point about Risky Business….

I respect that Holland America hires me often because of the consistent quality of my performance, I'm VERY mindful to always do my best work, never slack off…. But… every so often I get an idea for a new piece in my show that I really believe in and have to put it in… even though it may not be strong enough yet for a Holland America performance.

Conventional wisdom is to put a new piece in the middle of your act and surround it with strong material, so that if the weak piece really dies, it'll be buffered by strong material and the audience won't mind that. It's good advice and true. However, this new piece demanded I OPEN with it. So a new, untried piece of material opening the show and setting the tone for the entire performance. Normally I'd say no and keep working on it until I thought it was ready for HAL, but this time, I just had to say, What the fuck.

Turns out WTF did bring me freedom, and that new piece killed and opened the door to a killer show that night. It's part ability to perform and be funny on the fly… and part tremendous luck. I'm glad I did it though… and I'll keep on doing it. Sometimes, WTF moves you forward.

I'm off of ships now. It's all corporate performances and public shows from now on. I hope to see you out there.

Until next time, Good Night and Good Luck,
Jane Doe

Comedy Festivals

> *"Thing everyone loves about working comedy clubs is the audience tells you immediately if it's good or bad. No dickin' around, no mercy, no quarter. Tried a brand new thing tonight and boy, did they tell me. New material is painful, but no other way... if it kills first time out it's prolly shit anyway. So there. If you need me I'll be at the note pad...."*

That quote, in direct contradiction to my last thing about new material. Meh... contradiction is my essence. So, this week is full up with show-business weirdness; greed and crazy travel. Sit back, relax, throw the Clash on the turntable and listen to this.

Thursday, I drive from Toronto to Sarnia, roughly 4 hours, to be on a show at a high rollers golf tournament. That starts at 8pm. I'll be on by 9 pm and offstage by 10 pm if I'm lucky. I then HAVE to drive back to Toronto, getting me in around 2 am (if I'm lucky) so that I can sleep for a couple of hours and get on a plane at 7:30am to fly to Edmonton to start shows at the Edmonton Comedy Festival that night.

It was pure greed. I shouldn't have taken the Sarnia job, but I couldn't help myself. It's probably the last time this year I'll be at a golf tourney and I love to be around golf. The smell of the golf course is chock-full of memories for me. Additionally, the Edmonton Comedy festival is SUPER important... this is the first time they've ever headlined a variety comedian. The first time EVER. It means I have to have the best conceivable shows because if I don't, they'll never have a variety comedian again. The future of variety acts might sit on my shoulders, as it relates to this festival.

It's the weirdest thing. If a festival has a stand-up comedian, observational, long form, improv, whatever, and they die onstage, it's no big deal, they'll just book other comics next year. BUT, if a festival has variety and it doesn't work, or that act has a bad set for whatever reason, festival bookers ALWAYS say, "Well, variety doesn't work with our festival." Frankly, it's a load of shit. You just got an act who had a bad set, and that happens to EVERYONE time to time.

For me this week, it's a ton of pressure. I always push for festivals to have me, and I often leverage famous comedian friends to help me get them. A festival will never hire a variety act, no matter how funny, on their own. They need to get a push from the other comics, who basically say, "Yeah, it's ok to book a variety guy." In one sense I don't blame them for passing on variety. As someone who came up in comedy clubs I can tell you straight stand-up comics dislike variety... they just do. For a host of reasons mentioned earlier in this work. Point is, they don't like to work with us. I'm speaking of course in generalities. I know a TON of comics that like working with me and are happy to push for me… but they're in the minority. So I can see how festivals shy away from us, not wanting flak from the rest of the talent… but here's the thing: Variety comedy IS part of the comedy community. Like it or not, we represent a style of comedy. Comedy festivals are supposed to showcase ALL styles of stand-up. Especially if they're government-funded festivals. Excluding variety acts always struck me as odd, because it's by far the most popular kind of show. Variety comedy shows always sell out, even if people don't know the name of the performer. Audiences just like magic, and juggling, and mime, and other allied arts. Simple as that.

Anyway, that's this week. I come home Sunday for a couple of days then I spend a week on a ship, performing on their New England cruise. I leave from Halifax and go up the St. Lawrence to Boston, then on to Tampa and fly home. It's going to be a fantastic week. I really look forward to those shows.

Keep an eye out for me in your local airport, I'll be around, sitting in the lounge listening to Duanne Eddy's twangy guitar on the headphones before take-off.

See ya on the page, kids. Until then,
Good Night and Good Luck,
Jane Doe

Art or Craft

> *"An old magic routine was suggested to me to work on by a very well-read magician. He was right, it's up my alley. He asks, you know why it's good?*
>
> *Of course: it checks all the boxes of funny, magical, packs small plays big, no one's doing it, obscure.*
>
> *We also agree : magicians will gloss over the piece because there's lots of reading, no pictures, requires sleight-of-hand and requires you to imagine what you might do with it. No one will bother with the piece, despite its genius.*
>
> *Thinking about it while driving home, I wondered if the biggest problem facing magicians of late is simply... ease of use."*

I'm writing this largely to record my thinking at the time as much as anything else... here it comes.

Magic and comedy are NOT art. They cannot be. They never will be. The very nature of what makes both things technically work prevent them from being art. By its nature art is subjective. For something to be an artistic piece the viewer must be able to look at it and see many different things in and of it. Two people might look at a painting or a piece of dance or music or writing and get very different things from it. That's the brilliance of art. In comedy for a joke to work everyone in the audience must see the same thing. I have to paint a picture that the entire audience sees for the joke to technically work. They can't get different things from a punchline, they won't laugh. If everyone doesn't imagine the same thing I'm talking about they can't relate to the joke. That lag time in interpretation prevents the audience from laughing at once. The same holds true of magic. If I don't convince everyone in the theatre that they're seeing the same thing it cannot by definition be magic. If someone thinks I put a coin in my hand and another spectator doesn't see that, and instead sees it go into the other hand, I do not create magic. I create confusion. Everyone watching that magic effect has to see what the magician wants them to see, otherwise you're not fooling anyone. If thats happening you're not a magician. Either way it's just a craft. It can't be subjective.

True, you can express yourself in both forms. Using magic as a device to express a point of view can be done, but it's rare and very difficult. Still, that alone does not create art.

To my way of thinking magic and comedy are not art. They are craft to be sure, but not art. Like many other disciplines, magic and comedy both rely on formula, technique and other skills. That's a craft. Once the viewing public see anything other than what we are trying to make them see, it denatures the very thing we attempt to do. So, that's my two cents on that.

Tell me I'm wrong and why… have at it. Until then,
Good Night and Good Luck,
Jane Doe

Curtains Up

> *"I have to learn to be more optimistic. Last night the gig's sound didn't work, when it did it was inaudible, the physics of the room made any speech echo and muffled. Sightlines weren't great. No stage. Still, I had a really great show, and the people were wonderful. I just worked it old school, belted it out, slowly grabbing section by section until you have them all. The way I was taught. I'm too easily head faked, too negative about a show's potential when I'm faced with challenging conditions. It's also too easy to lose faith in one's skill set. It's not healthy to stew in negativity while waiting to go on. Point is, always be positive, even when faced with a potential shit show. Never know which way the sky will turn. Lessons from the road...."*

There's a moment right before the curtain opens and you walk out to perform for those thousand or 1500 audience members in the house. It's a short moment, maybe a second. You take a breath, and walk through that red crushed velvet wall, smile and go to work. That's my favourite moment of all things in professional show business performance.

I like the anticipation. Anything can happen. An audience decides if they like you in about 30 seconds. Those 30 seconds determine the strength of the show to follow. You better come out on that stage looking and acting like a million bucks. This is particularly true of comedy acts like myself. "Comedy Magician," they say, "what the hell is that?"

Have you ever heard it said that right before you die, in a single instant your life flashes before your eyes? That's sort of what happens when you take that big breath before you walk out from behind the curtain. In an instant the whole show, everything you hope to do that night, flashes before your eyes. That's the juice that keeps me going. it's as though I'm in the movie *Flatliners*, but for comedy and magic.

I leave this Friday for a week to perform on another ship out of Ft. Lauderdale. I'll be in Grand Cayman Island, Bahamas, Key West and Cozumel. It's a nice tour. After that I come home for a week and then I'm off for two more weeks, then on to Costa Rica, Hawaii and San Diego, on some other Dam ship (HAL joke... it's even on their shirts). It's the middle of winter here in Toronto, this is a blessing of a booking.

I hope to see you out there at sea. If you're in the audience that night take a moment to think of me, when the lights dim and I'm introduced. Right as they're saying my name, know that I'm focused. I'm taking that deep breath. Running over my show in a split second, hoping to make it the best show I can for me and most importantly... them.

Until then,
Good Night and Good Luck,
Jane Doe

Communication

> *"As a young act I used to think, "If I could just get on the TV show* Into The Night *with Rick Dees, my career would be set." Obviously means nothing. Point is, it takes a long while to come to the realization that all the media you chase is pretty temporary. The only thing that keeps you working is the act itself. Focus on that and you'll be fine. Everything else is gravy. On this, the Canadian Thanksgiving, I'm thankful for all the opportunities that came my way, and the people who gave me the chance to do what I wanted to do. I'm also thankful for the gravy. Lord help me, I ate so much gravy."*

A prominent and pretty famous magician, one whom I've admired since I was a kid, sent me a message not long ago. He'd seen me perform on the television show *Penn and Teller: Fool Us* and wanted to let me know that he very much enjoyed my performance and went on to say a few nice things about the jokes and the blocking of the piece. I was blown away. I've been watching this magician perform and create magic since I was very young. He's a borderline genius. To think he bothered to get his people to track down my email address and take the time to craft a note to me seems kind of madness, but there it is. It made my day that he wrote to me and it still makes me very happy when I think of it.

Until that email came in, I was feeling burnt out and unappreciated. This magician, who generously gave of his time, changed my mind and reinvigorated me to keep on plugging away in the business of show. Not the first time that's happened.

Hilariously, I didn't think I had that amazing a spot on the *Fool Us*, but this magician did. All this isn't to blow my own horn, but to make note of something pretty important. You never know to whom you may be important. Take the time to write a note to someone if you think they're doing something nice or doing good work. Maybe it'll change their lives. If nothing else you're keeping communication open between humans… how's that a bad thing?

Good night and Good Luck,
Jane Doe

All Roads Lead to Brampton

Fellow performers, a note. Performed tonight for a Tamil business group. As predicted, thinking about the food made my stomach growl loud enough for the mic to pick it up. Then, I mention during the show that I'm a HAM radio operator. Someone yells, 'Whats your callsign?' VA3MKF, I tell him, then take probably 3 or 4 minutes talking to this person about radio. It's so unprofessional to do so from the performing space, so selfish, but I couldn't help myself. The organizer said afterwards, 'I was going to jump in and stop the radio talk, but you guys seemed so genuinely interested in it, the audience actually liked it, it was truly memorable.'

This confirms my theory that if you talk about or do ANYTHING onstage that you're actually interested in, the audience will sense that and come along for the ride. Performers need to understand that more, I think.

You don't hear much about acts who take their shot and miss, but I'll tell you what happens to them. They end up working dead-end jobs on crazy shifts because they spent too much time chasing their dreams and not enough time preparing for what happens should that dream not come true. I was always taught to be mindful of that.

I grew up in Brampton, Ontario. A 45 minute drive from the centre of Toronto, Canada. By the time I was 16 I'd been performing magic for about four years at birthday parties, malls and libraries. That was all Brampton had to offer me.

Not long after my 16th birthday I was fortunate enough to win a comedy competition I'd read about in the local paper. Acts performed every week in elimination rounds until someone was the winner. Still in high school I lied about my age to enter. I combined magic and comedy into a set which, amazingly, won, not just the first night but overall. There were two "professional" judges for the final night. Agents who booked Harper's *A Little Night Magic,* Toronto's longest running magic dinner theatre, and the Laugh Resort Comedy Club in downtown Toronto. Both shows were in the same building. The dinner theatre on the main floor and comedy club four floors up. You'd need a sherpa to get up there. For winning the contest and surviving weeks of rounds of competition, I received the princely sum of 100 dollars, and a five-minute spot at the Laugh Resort. No sherpa.

There it was. Finally. I was going to get out of Brampton and into Toronto, where I would no doubt meet people like me, with the same interest in creating humorous magic. Surely upon my arrival at the club I'd meet the Andy Warhol of the Toronto magic scene and he would invite me to the magician version of The Factory and I could get on with being the Fran Lebowitz of magic.

No such luck.

I did the five-minute spot at the comedy club, and I died horribly.

Eric Tunney was the host that night and was very generous to me, as Eric was to everyone. I was young, awful, poorly dressed and had never really been out of Brampton to perform. I was nervous and unprepared. Fortunately, Doug Blakely, the booker for the magic dinner theatre and one of those comedy competition judges, had an interest in hiring me downstairs at the magic theatre. A young guy who would work cheap, who wouldn't want that? Still, a second chance presented itself. I really wanted the comedy club but the dinner theatre was pretty amazing too. Every act I'd read about or met at the magic shop performed there. A dream come true, to be honest. It was the best place to learn and get my performance chops. Performing regularly over a number of years put me on the path to a full-time career in comedy and magic, and along the way I became close to other working artists who remain friends to this day.

I recall my first night at *A Little Night Magic*. David Ben was performing close up, Glenn Ottaway was emcee, David Peck did the manipulation portion of the show and Ken and Barbie Poynter were closing with their illusions, all still friends to this day. First night there was my "audition" night. Doug was in the audience and a bunch of other acts came to see how new guy took the pressure. You could tell the theatre had a social clique amongst the acts and word must have spread fast about young guy coming in. I really wanted to be in that crowd. Sadly, I've never been "in" any crowd.

High Pressure.

Fold or hang tough. Call or raise the bet. These are decisions you make at the poker table. Sometimes the odds are stacked so clear there's only one way to play it. Other times you're best doing what's in your gut. That's very much how a showcase spot goes when it's something you really want. You never really know how exactly to play it until you're onstage. In my experience it's best to go with your gut. I got hired as an act at Harper's *A Little Night Magic*, mostly because I did what my gut told me to do.

Upon reflection, I have Doug Blakley and Jim Vanderburg (booker of the comedy club and second judge at the comedy competition) to thank for my career. They got me out of Brampton. They let a young kid play their venue and get much needed stage time and experience along the way.

"Earn while you learn," I like to say.

A little Night Magic led to the Laugh Resort, which led to Yuk Yuk's. That led to university gigs and then to corporate events. They led to performing at casinos in theatres and cruise ships around the world. From there it wasn't far to TV shows like *Penn and Teller: Fool US* and *America's Got Talent*. The booker from Yuk Yuk's left that organization and now handles most of my corporate work, he was comedian Russell Peters' manager at one time. Russell is a high school friend from Brampton. It's been a remarkably lucky ride, all spawning from Brampton. Were I of a religious nature I'd say I was blessed. Funny. It all started back at a little bar in Brampton, when a kid who dreamed of getting out of that life happened to win a comedy competition that no one ever heard of.

It's all pure luck, this career of mine. Anyone who says it's talent is lying. Talent has some but little to do with it. Luck, that's the name of the the show business game. I've never had to work a 9-5 for someone. I've only ever been an act. Traveling the world and getting paid for it. It's put me into a pretty comfortable life. Pure luck; even the friends you meet are pure luck.

As I said at the beginning, it's always best to prepare for taking your shot and missing. Money is important, but if you know me at all, you wouldn't be surprised to know I never followed that advice. I gave myself only one option: success. Failure just wasn't on the table because I have nothing else to fall back on. Showbiz IS my fallback. It's a pretty stupid play, since I now have a child and missus to look after. Neither of them work and I still have a mortgage. It could all come crashing down on me, if the luck of show business ever kicks out. It's happened to much better performers. Still, I think I'll keep swinging at it. If you consider where I started, I should never have come this far. So, lets see how far I can check it up. I'm no fan of not knowing how it's going to go, but I still love the thrill of performing, and all it takes is a single day for things to change for the better. Hard to give that up. I'm going with my gut.

Like papa Wallenda said, "Life is on the wire, the rest is just waiting."

Good night and good luck,
Jane Doe

Magic Shop

> *"We lost Marvyn Roy (Mr. Electric). He and his wife Carol were Liberace's opening act. They performed on* Sullivan *and many TV shows and theatres around the world. Showbiz royalty. I had the honour to perform with him front row when he came to the show at the theatre named after him in Palm Springs, California. He was SO nice, full of advice and stories. Great hang after the show. He always harped on how important it is to have an original act. He also talked about getting electrocuted occasionally with his act. That's suffering for your art. Still, he's the king. RIP man, and thank you!"*

Herb Morrissey of Morrissey Magic in Toronto passed away. I think he also caused the big Toronto blackout.

I miss him and the laughs at the shop and the advice along the way. The other day I put my foot up on a stool and lit a cigarette. Ha, I thought of Herb. Either you get that or you don't. Cans of coke, Chinese food from across the street and an unusual number of ashtrays on the counter. That's the magic shop of my youth. Good times. Herb and that magic shop were great to be around. 80's. Saturdays. Watching Herb demo Bob Farmer's latest thing, or refusing to demo something because the markup wasn't there. All the working acts hung out and talked shop. The best place to learn. Just timeless. I wonder what will happen to magic if the brick-and-mortar shops vanish. Not good things, I think.

I think you need a brick-and-mortar magic shop to hang out in, a place where someone can teach you things, where relationships are brokered and bits of your act are honed. Herb was the best for that. Often told me that a certain piece of material I was working on was complete garbage, but managed to point me towards something that would work better. It almost always was good advice, and some of the material I still do in my act today. In some regards, the magic shop does a better job of putting people on the path than a local magic club does.

We were lucky with Herb: He was a working act before he owned the shop. A manip act that played all the Playboy gentlemen's clubs around Montreal and, for a while, across the country. He and a ventriloquist friend named Gene Sneed, who also hung out at the shop, worked for decades and were at the top of their game. When advice came from either one of those guys, it was a good idea to listen.

I was lucky to have started in magic very young, and at the right time in the 80's. I was super lucky to live in Toronto where at the time two full-time magic shops operated; at one point there were 3. It was also a hotbed for magic too. Several famous magicians not only lived here but hung out at the shop. To have access to them, Herb, and the knowledge that came along with that was priceless. I'm not sure the internet will ever be able to compete with that. We'll have to see where the future of magic lies, but I'm certain the day of the brick-and-mortar magic shop is coming to a close. That's a shame. Acts won't have the same foundations to build on.

I can imagine Herb, hating the internet and everything it stood for, sitting at the shop, wondering how the hell society got to the point where no one reads a magic book, where magic was done on video for a non-existent audience, and no one set their sights on being a full-time act any more. Strange days.

Also: Magic Wand for sale, $250 (I wonder how many laymen tried to buy that exhaust pipe on the ceiling at the shop?).

Good Night and Good Luck,
Jane Doe

Road Memories

If Copperfield phones it in, he's still the best act on the strip. Phoning it in. Know why? Because he does more than 300 shows a year. He's the king.

When I was a kid I heard Lance Burton give the advice that to become really good you just have to do a lot of shows. Consistently. Always heard comics say it too. You only get good doing it a zillion times. Y'know why? Because you can't teach this. Not this type of performance. Gotta grind it out.

I was talking with a friend about her and her brothers' wild house parties in high school (cough cough… Gord Bennett… cough) she remarked I used to do magic at them for the insane drunks and wing nuts. Yea, I replied, you know what that gave me? Gift of being bulletproof. No crowd scared me after that. I could work anywhere. Point is, the lesson is to do a crap whack of shows for anyone, anywhere, when you're starting. Wow, it helps in ways you can't imagine. Don't even worry about the money. That'll come later.

The happiest times of my career working in the comedy industry are not, as many people would think, the gigs with international travel and performing at profile venues, on television or cruises.

Reality is, my all-time favourite memories are of a six-week period of the 90's when Ed Smeall was booker for the Yuk Yuk's chain of comedy clubs. By coincidence he'd booked me in a bunch of one-nighters every Saturday and Sunday. I think I still have the faxes of the gig sheets. Each one no more than two hours from Toronto. I'd get in the car, drive to the gig and on the way back, I was just close enough that I could listen to 102.1 CFNY broadcasting live from the Phoenix with 80's night. It was before iTunes and phones and I was always too lazy to make a zillion mix tapes. 80's night after the gigs, it was perfect. I could reflect on the performance that likely didn't go as well as I wanted, and still be made happy with the music. It was a real gift.

Sounds stupid, but I've never been as happy. I was working, learning, and I still got my 80's fix. By the time I got home my friends who were working at Kelsey's were just closing the bar and I could hang out with them for a while. What more could you want?

It's hard in the beginning, the "earn-while-you-learn" phase. You rely on the generosity of bookers putting up with your inconsistent performances.

You think you'll never be funny the way you want to be. I remember quite clearly working with Tom Stade at the Holiday Inn (I think Kingston) and marvelling at how he could be so effortlessly funny. It seemed impossible. In that period of several weeks I'd worked with Stewart Francis, Tom, Winston Spear, Sean Collins and a few others. It seemed impossible I could even approximate getting to their level. They were all so bloody funny.

Like the complete buffoon I am, I asked Tom one night, "How the hell do you do it like that?" To his credit he was super nice and gave the advice that now was so obvious: "You're not yourself up there yet, be yourself and everything else will follow."

It's the most important advice for performers. BE. YOURSELF.

It goes without saying that you should be original, creative with your language and do interesting material.... But in the end, if you're not yourself it'll all fall to shit. I never got to thank him for that advice, career-changing. He moved off to England and I haven't physically seen him since, even when I'm working there. You learn so much from watching the headliners as you're coming up. It's key. Sometimes I see the middle act leave, or the acts on early in the show leave, and I always think to myself, "You guys are missing out on a free education; wherever you have to go, I'd pass on it and stay here." You even learn from seeing someone die. In fact, you might learn more watching how to stickhandle that situation.

Tonight I'm performing at a resort in Belleville, about two hours from Toronto. I will honour the memory of those six-ish weeks by driving home blaring the music of The Specials, Murray Head, The B52's, The Bangles and the Box. Let's hope I don't recreate it too much and deliver a mediocre, middle-of-the-road show. Then again it's me, so one never knows. Beauty of comedy is, just when you think you have it figured out, you realize you don't fully know anything. You climb the mountain of shit to pluck the single rose, only to find out you've lost your sense of smell.

Thoughts from the road,
Good Night and Good Luck,
Jane Doe

Magicians: a Word of Caution

"Hustlers of the world, there's one mark you cannot beat: the mark inside."

—William S Burroughs

As a young man I had a falling out with a prominent magician. Quite an ugly falling out over, of all things, a table shuffle. A table faro shuffle. WOW.

I was a pretty fair close-up magician, but never what I did for a living. I'd have charitably listed myself slightly above average. Rarely performed that type of magic for money or audiences in general. The stage was where it was at for me. I loved it all the same, and since high school, few days passed that I didn't have a pack of cards in my hands and that I wasn't working on something. After that incident, that came to a close.

That falling out was so off-putting, so petty and childish, that I basically left the world of close-up magic for 10 or more years. In many ways it benefitted my stage work, allowing me to focus only on stagecraft. It is, after all, how I make my living and support my family. Still, it left a bitter taste in my mouth.

When I finally summoned the resolve to start working on close-up again, the Covid lockdowns happened, and that pretty much killed that. Another two years evaporated. Kid, house, loss of my stage performing career, it was really just survival mode. Even distractions didn't truly come together. Distractions like magic which, at any other low point in my life, would have been helpful, weren't. Now we're beyond it, once again I start the climb up the hill. It sucks. Sisyphus rolling the sponge ball up the hill. I've lost all touch with the cards I once had. Smoothness is gone, zero touch. I can't mechanically execute the things I once could with ease and precision and I've even forgotten the structure of classic effects that I thought were indelibly etched on my brain.

Working on something today out of an old book and simply not having the finesse, speed or recall of moves I know I should have, in an uncharacteristic fit of rage and frustration I threw the book across the room. In that moment I knew I no longer have the requisite skill set to be hanging out with the level of talent I often do. It's likely gone now. I feel like I'm back in high school starting over (I won't be buying any bloody packet tricks… fuck you, Nick Trost!). It saddens me. I can see the pieces, and where I might add a bit of business or touch of something here and there, but I don't have what it takes to be bringing that out in jam sessions or social settings. Truth is, I haven't had it for a long while. Evidence of that is peppered across meetings with other acts over the years.

It's not that I perform effects like a stroke victim or something, but I'm just not that sharp anymore.

You might say that if I were that easily put off something I was so passionate about, that if a dispute with another magician kicked me off the wagon, I wasn't tough enough to want it badly anyway. You hear that levelled at young comedians at amateur night. The determined ones survive and come back. A fair point, and it's not lost on me. I defend abandoning close-up by reminding myself that I was young and this was an established, well-known act, respected by the world (I think). Published. A baller. Always disappointing seeing the powerful in an industry be shitty. Still, I can't help feel there's a pettiness about the arts that drives this kind of thing. I used to spend a lot of time being angry with that magician and the whole shuffle incident. I realize now I only have myself to blame. I should have kept on truckin'.

Here's the point of this long diatribe directed largely at the younger talent: Don't let ANYONE or ANYTHING steal from you the thing from which you take joy. If you think you're doing work you're happy with, run with it. Never let anything have the kind of power over you to end it, because you'll be resentful when it's gone.

Time and talent are the only commodities we have in this bankrupt world, so don't give up any of it to nonsense.

Try to remember that, even the people you think know a ton, probably don't know shit from good chocolate.

Tips from the stage and the (ex-)close-up Matt,
Good Night and Good Luck,
Jane Doe

Price

A thought, since price is often a topic of discussion amongst us.... This is a price list from a Toronto entertainment agency. 1993, almost 30 years ago. Most of us listed here are still working today.... If your fee isn't higher now than what we were charging 30 years back, maybe you ought to rethink your fees. All boats would rise.... For the record, flyer is from Golden Canadian Productions. Gave me a ton of work as a kid. Gave me a career, really. But I lied. I never had doves. Fuck that shit.

I lost a gig to a guy 30 grand more than me. I'm gonna tell you a show business secret. For some reason, no one seems to want this fact out there but, if I drop dead tomorrow (seems likely) maybe someone will scroll through my book in the future and learn the lesson it took me ages to accept.

To be transparent, I wasn't undercutting the market. Straight up, I was asking a middle of the road 10. The producer said she WANTED me to have the gig, she WANTED it to happen for me. So why didn't she swing for the fences for me on this one, I ask politely, already knowing the answer? She says flatly, "He was more money, therefore there's more incentive for me to book him at 40 than you at 10."

Simple.

Talent buyers WORK ON COMMISSION, and they often split that commission with other people working on the event. She said "I gave you every opportunity, every chance, I told you who was on the pitch." Roughly translated, that means I knew the approximate price of everyone involved and should have quoted accordingly. I didn't, because I'm stupid, distracted and wasn't thinking.

The commission thing is only partly the lesson. The real lesson is everything in show business operates not on reality, but the PERCEPTION of reality. I don't care who it is, when compared to some poor person working outside in the cold on the tools 12 hours a day, ain't no act in Canada is legit worth 40 grand for 35 min of show... but it happens. All the time. Ya just gotta big yourself up a bit. Be your own hype man for a while. Be Flava Flav to your Public Enemy. BRING THE NOISE... !

The money is out there, why let someone else get it? YOU are worth the money. If you're a solid act, you're worth it. Talent buyers want to pay you more so they make more. Don't doubt yourself. In fact, you'll often lose gigs or never be considered for them if you're too cheap.

Believe in yourself and your work. You put years of work into this thing, so get paid for that experience. Know what I mean? You can tell me I'm full of shit, there's no consistent market, etc., etc.... I used to say that too when I was younger, and older acts would tell me this. It's not bullshit, there's a big market out there with all sorts of money to spend on stupid stuff like a funny guy with a rubber chicken.

Think about it, event with 800 people pays 95 bucks a plate for food, thats 76 grand in food, then there's AV, decor, etc., etc. I mean... surely you, as the headline entertainment, the thing everyone remembers for the night, should be worth at least a percentage of what they spend on crappy chicken. You ever attend an event and talk the next day about the chicken? No, it's what the entertainment was. Keep that in mind, man.

I'll take all sorts of heat for this. For all sorts of reasons. Acts are squirrely, I don't care anymore. I'm semi-retired. I'm just putting it out there, for the record, because I hear the printed page doesn't forget. When I'm dead, if this helps but one act, I'll be thrilled. It's hard to let go the lower paying stuff and go after the better paying stuff. It's hard because you don't know if you'll get it, and if you stay at the lower price you fear you'll lose that AND the higher end stuff too. It's in your head, that's all. Like thinking the hot person at the bar won't talk to you because you're not hot enough. Confidence wins the day. Put the clock around your neck, get on the Viking horns, and hype. We work in the business of bullshit; leverage it.

To close, here's the best part... all boats rise if everyone shoots higher up. We ALL do better. We all make more money, get better working conditions, have more time to do other stuff... like build Lego.

Just something to think on.

Thoughts from the workhouse.
Good Night and Good Luck,
Jane Doe

Strategy of Covid

June 29, 2020

(To remind you how acts felt 3 months in)

Show business is chess. It isn't checkers. Everything is long game. So maybe this is a bad play. It's hard to say what to do.

I've been performing in this business of show full time, never having a job or anyone to split a household bill with me for 30 years. An exceptional run, by any standards. I often say show business has been very good to me, better than I deserve. But that's a lie. I'm a damn good act, and I know my work. I've earned what I've achieved. I'm a good magician and comedian. That said, at this 100+ days into Covid with it crushing show business, venues, and showing no signs of stopping. It appears my career is over. The reality is that, while there are some virtual shows to be had, there are not enough. None at a high paying enough price point to create a real living. Sure, there are outliers, ones who've made 140k virtual in a night, but that's rare. The bigger shows that will facilitate that income won't be back for over a year. It's likely more and it's already been almost 4 months. The reality is, it will have been 2 years without work by the end of it. What's a real income?

I have no spouse with a job, or family money or side hustle cash coming in. That means it has to be an income that supports my house (which I owe very little on), a car (which is paid for) and its variety of bills, household bills, and something that resembles savings for emergencies and for retirement (HA! like that will happen). Chief responsibility above all of those things is the 5-year old and the other adult in this house who depend on me to pay those bills, and to provide a safe, stable future with reasonable expectation food will be on the table and as normal a life as can be had when they're attached to a touring performer. To that end, it seems show business was generous enough to let me have 30 great years. Years being paid to travel the planet and appear on television, radio, theatres and cruise ships. It was pretty great, in fact it was not just a career I love, it's the only one I ever really wanted. It could be that's over now and maybe I should jump ahead of it. I started in the late 1980's / early 90's recession. I've fought back that, and the tech collapse in '98, then 9/11, then the 2008 collapse. Losing work, money and momentum each time. EVERY FUCKING TIME. But I kept going because this is the job I love and I didn't swim this far out to sea to save anything for the swim back. I'm starting to look back to shore now.

For the first time since I was 16 years old, I think, MAYBE I will begin the process of looking for a job. That statement sickens me and is profoundly soul-crushing. There is no way for me to describe exactly how that feels. There isn't. You might have lost a job at one point, and think you know, but you don't. A career in the arts is very different and I'm not just saying that. Yes, I'm sure you've had a job your whole life. Me too, mine was really different than yours. If you think after a lifetime of performing and beating a nearly impossible business with odds so crazily stacked against you, and building relationships and a successful business, and be one of the select few that are good enough to be paid to travel the world to share your work… if you think that it's not a giant kick in the yam bag to have to give that up and go out to look for a day job, at 46… you'd be wrong. When I think about it, literally, it's hard to breathe. The worst thing that could happen is to ride this Covid waiting game out too long and have to make decisions last minute. Too many people and physical things depend on me to roll those dice. The arts have taught me one valuable lesson, and that is to never make decisions from a position of panic and weakness. So, while I still have money enough to survive for quite a while longer, is it best to get ahead of this? Email me and tell me what you think… I honestly don't know. I have no marketable skills. At least none anyone would hire on without work experience. I toured with a comic named Hal Spear. He passed away, but I remember him having to get a day job at one point. It was when show business crapped out on him. I asked what that was like. His reply was ,"It makes you feel very small." Originally, I took that to mean that somehow, a day job, working for someone, was "less" than what we do and not honourable. I didn't care for that position at all.

Now I see what he really meant. He meant, I think, that you're used to being the centre of attention while you're onstage, and there's a faux glamour that comes with being flown around, paid handsomely to travel and perform. Life is on the wire, papa Wallenda says, the rest is waiting. It wasn't a shot against working people, it's just that it's a way of working that we've never even considered and, holy crap, it's hard, and you're often ignored. You feel small because you realize how good you've had it all this time working in the business of show. Covid calls checkmate.

Until I see you in the park with Bobby Fisher,
Good Night and Good Luck,
Jane Doe

Artists are in trouble

A Pandemic Post 2

(originally published for the public, submitted for perspective)

I want to pass this along for consideration. Early morning I had to talk an artist out of punching their ticket. You never want someone to check out of the world that way. Believe me when I tell you, that's not an easy phone conversation. A lot at risk. I smoked a lot during that call, the one time I could NOT screw things up. It's ok now, so far, they'll be alright… but there's some take-aways I hadn't thought of. If you come across a situation like this, here are some things I learned that you may not have considered. For empathy's sake, it's this.

A lot of artists are facing losing their homes. None of us are working now. Some of us are lucky enough to own a house, and when savings run out, it's likely a line of credit can be used. When that runs out, roll that into the mortgage… rinse, repeat, assuming banks are willing to lend. Not a great option, but an option.

Things are different: MANY artists are out of savings RIGHT NOW. I'm talking zero cash. They never made much to begin with and banks won't lend to them. They rent, not own. There is no equity to tap. They face losing their apartments, and when the CERB runs out, which for many will be early June, there will be nothing. It's homeless time. Welfare isn't enough to rent anything in Toronto. It's homeless shelter time. Some artists have kids too. Imagine that pressure. You think they should have saved for the rainy day?

Well, it's a torrential downpour now. I'd like to remind you that this happened for artists during the tech bubble bursting, 9/11, 2008 economic collapse, and now again. Assuming they had no relationships or divorce that cost them more… that's still a lot of savings to burn through, weathering those storms. I mean, how much should they have saved? Remember, they have no pension or benefits. A dental bill could send them into an economic tail spin. There's nothing left to beat this back with. Likely artistic work won't come back for 18 months. Maybe more. Speakers, performers, hospitality sector, hotel workers, etc., it's gone for them all. However, the artists aren't trained for anything, even retail work. Be mindful of that. Arts people are out of options.

Try not to judge. Jobs are scarce. Not that artists are trained for much but the service sector jobs will be fought over by students, retirees who didn't save enough along the way, and… artists. It goes on and on, you can see….

The point is MANY, nearly all, artists are under pressure that people who have pensions, benefits and jobs don't even think about and can't imagine. Even if you just have a job, you probably don't consider how bleak the future is if you're in the arts. Try and imagine you're in your 40's or 50's or more and you've burned through savings just getting to here, with no hope of work on the horizon and facing homelessness.... The stress of it all is breathtaking. What I'm saying is: Have some empathy. Don't be surprised if artists you know or see on Facebook are snapping or lashing out or posting desperate, angry stuff. Be mindful of how they feel. Listen. For artists right now, especially ones who interact with people or depend on the theatre, this is worse than the Great Depression. Very little chance of things returning to any kind of normal. Don't tell them to pivot, don't offer that kind of advice. Most of it is useless anyway. Next time I hear the word pivot I'm gonna punch someone in the junk. It's not helpful right now, that type of advice. I worry there's going to be a crap whack of artists who will simply kill themselves because there isn't hope, or they think they're worth more dead than alive to their family. If you thought AIDS gutted the arts community in the 80's, that's going to seem like a drop in the bucket compared to this. We have to do something. I just haven't got a friggin' clue what that is. Remember that during the worst of this pandemic as you binge-watched TV and read books to help pass the time and keep you sane, it was to the artists you turned to for help. So, who do they turn to for immediate help now?

Thoughts from the workhouses,
Good Night and Good Luck,
Jane Doe

Old Friends

Turns out I killed at that Amish gig last night. Shocker. Sometimes you surprise yourself. Goes to show the old school advice never doesn't apply. The magic is YOU, it's only you. Be charming, confident, but at the same time, self-deprecating. Work the room slowly until you have them all, one at a time if you have to. Don't rush. If need be, get them talking to you, you'll find common ground everyone can relate to and you're in. A big thanks to all the comics and magicians who taught me these and countless other lessons along the way. You always owe your career to them, even if they didn't know it. They gave you the tools to figure it all out. That's never for one second lost on me. Hope there's some tools in here for you.

Dave Hook was a good comic. I miss him a ton. We started about the same time, and while I worked with him a bit at Yuk Yuk's, I really got to know him from "outside gigs." We did a local tv show together in support of charity. They were recording the whole comedy show for broadcast. I go up, do my thing, another comic, then Hook. He got third position, the sweet spot.

A couple minutes into his set Hook does a joke about Ronald McDonald and some guy in the audience freaks out. Just loses his mind, right there on camera. He's yelling at Dave about how Ronald McDonald House saved his dying son and how Hook is a giant ass… it was epic heckling. Dave took it all in stride, nodding his head and finally said, "Sir, I'm so sorry man, we're just here for some laughs, let's just move on with the show. I'm sorry, really I am (Dave picks up his guitar and goes on). I didn't wanna make fun of your kid, or his situation. Let me just play a song and move on. Dave strums the guitar once. I honestly think he's trying to save the set, knowing they can edit out the heckler. Brrring, goes the guitar, and then he sings:

RONALD MCDONALD FUCKS KIDS!!! RONALD MCDONALD FUCKS KIDS!!!

Omg. Not sure I ever laughed so hard in my life. Audience guy blows a gasket. Hook, zero fucks given. RIP Dave. So many good road stories with you. Thanks. Also, I think of you every single time I walk into a McDonalds.

Good Night and Good Luck,
Jane Doe

Entertaining in the Heat

I think having happy performing conditions makes the show better. That could be weather, food, extra toilet paper. Whatever your jam is, mindset is everything.

If I were a character in the Rankin Bass holiday classic, *A Year Without A Santa Claus*, I'd without question be Heat Miser.

I work primarily with two entertainment agencies, one here in Toronto and the other in L.A. Both specialize in pairing niche entertainment services like mine, an interactive comedy and magic show, with the right clients. They're both wonderful to work with. Los Angeles is warm, Toronto is not. It's no secret to either agent that I hate the winter and the snow especially. Both agencies are generous enough to try and book me at events in climates where there's no snow. For most comedians and magicians, December is busy with corporate holiday parties. I've never been the type of act that wanted to churn out 50 shows in a month, so I take a select few holiday parties for corporations that really enjoy what I do and with whom I like to work. Sadly, this month, try as the agents might, I have no bookings in warm climates for December OR January. All my performances are in places like Winnipeg and London, where the cold lives and multiplies. I shouldn't complain, of course, they're good-paying gigs with great conditions and for companies that many entertainers would kill to work for. I'm not complaining, I'm really not. As always I'm super grateful. It's just, I wish… I wish that in January or February, a cruise ship booking would come along from one of the lines I love to work, like Holland America or Princess, to break up the winter, or perhaps a conference in Miami or Vancouver. Here's the thing: Continuing to perform and being able to support my family is paramount. I'll perform on the frozen dark side of the moon, get no Air Miles and bring my own mic if it means supporting them. But if I could choose…. Sure would be nice to get something, somewhere warm. So… if by some strange twist of fate you're reading this and you're in Vancouver, the Island… anywhere that snow isn't a concern and you have a conference or convention coming up, or any event where there's a meal, people are seated and afterwards could use some entertainment to cap the day off, let's talk. I think I can arrange a warm climate deal for you if it means getting me out of the frozen hell of Hoth that I'm currently in. I could also of course just book a vacation… there's that.

Until then,
Good Night and Good Luck,
Jane Doe

Generosity of Spirit

"Some people are just beautifully wrapped boxes of shit."

Arlene Dickinson, star of *Dragon's Den* and one of Canada's foremost entrepreneurs, got a weird bit of press the other day. I came across it on the net while looking up memories from an old tour. It basically suggested that, for all her fame and money, the notion of her helping people is nothing more than a façade. A way to generate more money for her. Meh. Let me tell you a story about that, because I'd like to say otherwise.

I was on a show tour to Europe and the Middle East with Arlene Dickinson, hockey legend Tiger Williams, country music star Tim Hicks, some famous NHL and CFL athletes (like I know anything about sports) and a female singer, new-ish to the business but connected up with Tim and a few other people. You could see she's on her way up. She wasn't shy in the talent department, that's for sure. We flew on the Prime Minister of Canada's plane, which we had to ourselves. About 20 of us. Talent, crew, athletes and no one else. Pretty cool.

Here's the thing: After we left Belgium, en route to Italy for the next set of shows (on the back of a battleship, can you imagine!), a bit of a jam session broke out in the the plane. Microphone, lighting, instruments, you name it, got pulled from cargo and set up in the back of the aircraft. It was pretty epic. A live show, just for the crew and NHL athletes and military escorts on the plane at 35,000 feet. A career first for me. I did a spot, killed.... Tim Hicks CRUSHES it with two of his original songs, "Stronger Beer" being one, then a requested cover. Then the other singer, who I don't feel the need to name, went up and did two cover songs. She's ridiculously talented but did covers in both the airplane show and the live shows at venues on the ground. Still, she was epic. Everyone loved her.

Arlene comes up to me after the show and says really nice things about my set and that I'm funny. She was genuine about it. A pro to be sure, I believed she meant the really nice things she was saying. I've never used it as a pull quote for promotional purposes; I just like that she said it. She was like that with everybody. Then I saw her do something I thought was profoundly generous. Arlene went up to the singer who did the cover songs and told her she was tremendously talented. She instinctively knew the things that artist needed to hear. Made her feel really special. Then Arlene asked why she sang cover songs. Did she have any of her own work? Singer said she did, but had no luck getting it produced and wasn't sure of the quality. Typical artist talk I guess, lacking self-confidence. Then Arlene says, "You know, you'd benefit from talking to one of my friends. Sarah McLaughlin and I are close. I'll call her and set up a chat with her. Between her and I we can help you get to where you need to go."

As I stood there, I thought to myself that this was just BS showbiz talk. People are always saying they're going to help you and don't. This is especially true of celebrities and the wealthy you work with. It occurred to me that the singer would feel really happy in the moment, but when the tour is over and no call from Sarah McLaughlin comes, she'll feel the sting of show business. Always a tough blow.

Then it happened. Arlene picks up the air phone and calls Sarah. Yup, the AIR PHONE. Yeah, that's right, at 35 thousand feet… just calls Sarah McLaughlin, on her cell… tells her the situation with this singer, and asks if she can help. Something was said on the other end of the phone, then Arlene hands over the phone and says, "Sarah wants to talk to you, ask her anything you like and take as much time as you need."

That happened…. And much more. Here's the point of it. Arlene didn't GET anything from that transaction other than helping out an artist and human being she thought had talent. That's generous, charitable and with no ulterior motive. I think that's the kind of person she is. I've watched her with people quite a bit on that two-week tour. It's how she rolls. When I read that Arlene is somehow selfish and out to just make herself money at the expense of others, I think of this story. I think completely the opposite. From my relationships with her, I just don't see it. She doesn't need MORE money, that's not the driving factor anymore. She just wants to help people where she can. I'm no one… who's gonna listen, but I feel it's necessary to put it out there. My experience is not what I read on the internet in that post. I think she's a genuinely good person who cares about people and her family and remembers what it's like to struggle.

On the way home, we were delayed going into Ottawa to make connections to Toronto. She once again got on the air phone from the military plane and called Air Canada… said we were coming in from an Armed Forces tour and used her celebrity status to get them to hold the plane, check our bags and tag them through without us even being there. It was a really nice thing. I only had one night at home with my family before I had to fly out for another tour. Had I missed that connection I wouldn't have seen them. She made that happen. I'm eternally grateful. The elevator has gone all the way up to the top for Arlene and she clearly feels the need to send it back down to help others waiting to take the ride up. Remember that, should you ever find yourself at the top floor. Just my 2 cents, Good Night and Good Luck, Jane Doe

Where in the World is Matt?

Submitted purely for ego....

My big dream was one day of visiting everywhere in the world that was mentioned on the opening credits of *Where in the World is Carmen Sandiego?*. Wow, I loved that show! After three decades of performing full time at corporate events, headlining cruise ships and casinos and just about any venue you can name, it's finally happened. I've been to EVERYWHERE in the world Carmen Sandiego has been. It's epic and quite a huge thing for me. Magic gave me that. I owe magic a lot. I owe it a debt of gratitude. If I were pressed on it I'd say I've left magic better than when I found it. I'm proud of that, but I'm also insanely thankful to it for everything magic has done for me. It's done SO much for me and now it's let me round out my childhood dream. See ya on the road! Good Night and Good Luck, Jane Doe

P.S. If you want the lyrics to the song by Rockapella, here it is:

Well she sneaks around the world from Kiev to Carolina
She's a sticky-fingered filcher from Berlin down to Belize
She'll take you for a ride on a slow boat to China
Tell me where in the world is Carmen Sandiego?

Steal their Seoul in South Korea, make Antarctica cry Uncle
From the Red Sea to Greenland they'll be singing the blues
Well they never Arkansas her steal the Mekong from the jungle
Tell me where in the world is Carmen Sandiego?

She go from Nashville to Norway, Bonaire to Zimbabwe
Chicago to Czechoslovakia and back!

Well she'll ransack Pakistan and run a scam in Scandinavia
Then she'll stick 'em up Down Under and go pick-pocket Perth
She put the Miss in misdemeanour when she stole the beans from Lima
Tell me where in the world is Carmen Sandiego?
Oh tell me where in the world is, oh tell me where can she be?

Ooh, Botswana to Thailand, Milan via Amsterdam
Mali to Bali, Ohio, Oahu!
Oh, tell me where in the world is Carmen Sandiego?

Inconvenient Truths About Hiring Entertainment

Here's how the roller coaster of the performer mind works. Photographer sends pics from a show. I look and think, 'Wow I'm fat, my face looks fat, I have to tell photographers in the future how to shoot me.' Then you have to shift and return to your resting state of self-loathing and you think, 'Or you could just lose weight, you fat fuck.' This goes back and forth until finally, you close the photo files and return to working on your taxes. Then you think about the hair you're losing.... Point is, don't let yourself fall into this trap like I have, my whole damn life.

Artists say they specialize, that they're corporate professionals. Very often, they simply are not. They make that claim because they believe money is to be made working with companies. They're just after another revenue stream. I don't think that's what you want for entertainment. You need to hire a specialist, a MacGyver in the world of talent. Someone who can troubleshoot onsite and deliver results. Professionals cost money, it's true. You likely wonder if I'm one of those professionals or just someone saying that I am. Legitimate question and tough to answer, especially with the state of the internet. The entertainer you hire reflects on your job, your company, you personally and your event. Making a wise choice is tough. 100%.... I get it. Am I the person to hire? I know that I am, but consider this: even if you don't book me...

... hire only entertainers who truly focus on specific performance. Corporate performance, for your demographic. Google the name of the act you're looking at. If you see they also perform for unrelated events, that's a concern. A corporate performer may also work on luxury cruise lines but won't be working for children or bar events. They won't scatter their efforts. These artists will know other pros, planners and bureaus in the market. If industry people haven't heard of that act, that's a red flag, so look to see if they're represented and talked about. Google will show all of that. They will have a long history with this work. More than video, more than anything, look at the quotes from other companies like yours. References count. Contact the entertainer and ask for those letters of reference or for permission to talk to past clients. Any act who's appropriate for your event will have those available.

Here's the truth about promotional video. It's hard to get footage from a show that truly captures the best of an artist at a corporate function. The video of the concert you saw, the YouTube clip of your favourite band, simply will not stand up to seeing them live. Think of a show you saw live, then

YouTube that show and have a look. Doesn't come close, does it? That's how video deceives buyers. It's also why so many promotional videos are edited quickly, they have to be because there's no way to recreate the LIVE experience. The nature of comedic and visual interactive performers demands it be seen in real time; video will never tell you the truth. With that in mind, know that video won't capture the power of what you're after. It's important to speak to other clients of that artist, similar to your industry, who've hired that act. Someone who can explain the connection that performer made with the audience. Believe in that. If the artist you're looking at can't supply you with those references, forget about them. Period.

I own "Take the Boredom out of the Boardroom." That's my slogan; and what I mean by that is, any meeting or conference or convention you attend or host, I can make fun and memorable. That's ALL I do. I specialize. If your event has people seated, I'm the perfect fit to cap off that event. My clients will speak to that. I don't have fancy edited video. I don't "speak" on topics. I don't have metaphors for thinking like a magician. I don't have PowerPoint. What I DO have is a sold block of entertainment you can be sure will be a success and reflect well on you and your decision to book me. I have the references to back that claim up. I have years of experience. I've worked on creating performances for functions like yours.

Yes, I've performed on Penn and Teller's TV show and been interviewed on CBC Radio and appeared at comedy festivals. I was fortunate to be invited on those programs and they lend credibility and prestige to my show, but they are ancillary to my core work, being a corporate entertainment professional. Know that I believe great shows for happy clients make for a healthy entertainment community. More than anything, that's what I want. All boats rise when things run smoothly, and that's what we should all hope for. Think about where ya want to work and focus on it.

Until I see you from the stage,
Good Night and Good Luck,
Jane Doe

Charity Event

Stand-up comedy, the business of making people laugh in a group, was always arithmetic. Formula, personality, crowds reacting in a certain way because of setting and conditions, how they're seated, temperature of the space, the general mood of society... it goes on and on... they all play into why people laugh in a room. It's NOT simple, trust me.

I'm performing at a charity event in Caledon, Ontario next week. It's rare for me to perform at these types of events, since my schedule with corporate conference- and convention performing, cruise ships and casinos rarely affords me the time to do something to help the community. It's troubling because these are often the causes I believe in most. In this particular case, MY community is involved. Fortunately, I have time for this one and I'm glad. As a comedian and magician, especially someone focused on being attractive to corporate audiences, it's easy to forget there are worthy causes out there that also need the attention of performers. Of course, I'm paid to perform at these charity events; you should never work for free, but I give them a reduced rate and try to leverage my presence at the event to generate some media attention for their cause. It's what we can do, more to come on that. If it's a cause I believe in, I want to work with them and use whatever tiny bit of celebrity I have to aid that cause.

My point is that not everything in life revolves around money. You need to help out when you can. In this regard, I'm pretty left leaning. I mean.... What's wrong with the world? Money. Evil defence contractors have it, noble causes do not. Money's greatest ability is to continue letting bad people do bad things at the expense of those who don't have any. So, when the chance comes along to help out the noble causes, let's swing for the fences and do what we can. I look forward to seeing you out there at my shows, public and private.

Until then....
Good Night and Good Luck,
Jane Doe

Comfort Zone

When I was in high school I performed on my first cruise ship. Just over 30-day contract. Worst / best experience ever. It was the first and LAST time I ever wore a name tag. I am grateful that experience taught me early in my career the shit I will NEVER put up with again. Rumour was I set fire to, and blew up the car of the talent agent who booked this ship because he didn't pay me for a month of shows and overworked all the acts and denied paying my airfare home. Well, I refuse to confirm that story but it was the first and last time I ever wore a name tag. Never again. Never. Like Tron, I fight for the users.

All I can say is there's more to blowing up a car than the movies make it seem. One does not simply stick a rag into the gas tank and light it. It's a lot of work. Do I look like the kind of guy who'd research all that, just for revenge ?"

Jeff McBride says, "Your comfort zone is the place your dreams go to die." I think he's correct. I'm currently ¾ of the way through writing a new closing piece for the show. I know it sounds insane to plunk in a new closer without audience-testing it elsewhere in the show, but here's the thing: It's not a comedy piece. There's zero jokes in it. It's not even the strongest magic in the show. However, it needs to be at the end. It MUST be.

That's right, I intend to close my comedy magic show with an autobiographical performance piece. It will neither rely on jokes nor magic. The departure from the norm is huge for me. It will be a whole new performing chop, one I'm looking forward to growing. At 44 years old, I think I'm finally ready to start letting the audience see more of me than ever before.

To give you a notion of where it's heading, the piece begins with "My mom is the toughest person I know. As if the jackboot of the patriarchy pushing down on her wasn't enough to make life intolerable, my dad died when I was young…."

I know you're going to say: This will surely kill all the comedy momentum I've built up to that point… but I'm not sure that's true. Do they really need to be laughing til tears right at the end? My now second-to-the-end of the show is the underwear piece… my former closer. That's a killer. I can often get a standing O on that. They're laughing til tears then. Why not shift the beat to something real, and have them leave on a real moment? The show has nothing about ME to any degree. The audience leaves being entertained but not knowing about ME. I'd like to change that. I want to connect with them more.

It's my belief (and we'll see in the next few months if this is true) to really, genuinely connect with an audience and have them feel anything of value, you need be honest and really speak to them. So, I'll wow and entertain them along the way, I'll talk about my son and my home a bit… then after the underwear piece, I'll use the last 3 minutes of the show for a short performance driven closer.

I recently noticed that when I started talking about my son while I was on stage, days later people would come up to me in public to tell me they liked the show and all that jazz… but they would also mention Ferris, my son. They'd often call him by name and ask about him. That's when I realized, just briefly talking about my kid connects with an audience, maybe more than anything else I do. So simple. So true. I never realized it. I was too busy coming up with clever jokes. I missed the forest for the trees.

The point is this. Grow or die. Your audience needs to see more of you on stage. Connect with them, it's what people are paying that ticket price for. I don't mean that Copperfield bullshit about how you never saw it snow when you were a kid. I mean, the closer to the bone of who you really are will be the thing that gets you across the finish line.

When people come back to buy a ticket for my show, or return to a cruise ship to see my performance, I don't want them saying, "I can't wait to see that comedy magic guy" or "I can't wait to see that comedian," I want them saying, "I can't wait to see Matt DiSero again, I wonder what's up with his life." Never be a generic thing… always be you. You never want them to hire a magician. You want them to hire YOU. It's a lesson I learned a long time ago and didn't implement until only few years ago. It was a tragic waste of time. Like Goshman always said, "The Magic is YOU!"

So… sit back, grab a glass of scotch, throw on The Cure. Pick a cool track like "Fascination Street" and write some new stuff…. You'll be thankful you did and closer to the artist you want to be.

Until next time,
Good Night and Good Luck,
Jane Doe

Ricky Jay

"There is only one thing I fear in life, my friend: One day, the black will swallow the red."

—Mark Rothko

I'm sitting here at a friend's house, looking at the iconic photo Richard Avedon took of Ricky Jay, the original print. It's staggeringly interesting. Avedon was a master at getting to the heart of a subject. He was a true genius. I'm a fan of many artists. Especially of a certain era, some were super cool and had lots to say, painters and photographers chief among them. Specifically Richard Avedon and Peter Hujar, Anne Sexton, Dorothy Parker, I could go on.... I'm a sucker for writers and poets and filmmakers and even magicians. I like artists of a certain sensibility. Ricky Jay was one of those artists.

Ricky died Nov 24th, 2018. No idea what the circumstances surrounding his death are. I sure hope he didn't go the way of Mark Rothko. Ricky had a profound effect on magic, a true game changer. One of the greatest exponents of the craft and a wonderfully charming and interesting personality onstage. No mere magician, he was Ricky Jay, — Author, Magician, Actor, Consultant and Raconteur.

I'll leave it to whoever may be reading this to search out and view his work if you're not familiar, it's not hard to find. An HBO special about him is one of the better works. You should have to work a bit to suss out great artists, so check out all his work if you can.

I guess I just wanted to say this: The greatest artists in every field leave a body of work that's timeless and that people will absorb and enjoy forever. Ricky's work is like that. He raised the bar to a level to which we should all aspire. There will now be more copycat Ricky Jay acts, death of the greats seems to bring that out... but, there it is. I don't think he would approve of that but Ricky would like it, I think, if we all took magic somewhere it wasn't before. It is, in the end, the job of an artist to do that.

Until I see you out on the page,
Good Night and Good Luck,
Jane Doe

Sweep the Leg

Norm Macdonald and I do a gig together in Ohio. Corporate thing, but he'd just come off SNL. Naturally he's closing. I go out and do my little song and dance, crowd loves it but it's corporate, so... is what it is. Honestly, it's Norm they want. He goes out and does some super dark stuff. I freely admit it was hilarious but not suitable for corporate.

From behind the curtain I can see swaths of people getting up and leaving. A bank of 20 people. Then another of 40. Then what appears to be a whole row of people. Like that. 25 or 30 min in he's lost 70 percent of the crowd. He stops, squares to the mic and says, "Hey, what'd you expect me to do? Jokes about losing my luggage?"

Everyone wants to know how to get more work. I always say I work a lot because the universe allows me to. I think a big part of my success or lack of success is because the universe says so. There's some other things too.... I regularly get emails from other acts asking me how to get on cruise ships, or work more corporate. The answer no one ever wants to hear is the only answer: Be really good. As Steve Martin says, "Be so good they can't ignore you."

It's true. Being great gets you all the work.

Here's my two cents on this. Sometimes, you gotta Sweep the Leg. It's hard to stand back and look objectively at your act. So, do one of two things. Hire a director, coach or comedy writer to help with those things, or have industry friends you trust watch your videos and see your shows and have them make suggestions. I've taken both approaches and both are useful. If you're going the friend route, make sure it's someone you trust and someone who's better than you. If they're at the same level or not doing as well, why get the advice?

Look, I'm a corporate act. I'm not changing the world here, but I do want my work to be the best it can be. Christmas and holiday parties are coming up, I want to work too. I want to work but there's only one way to get that work. Just kill every show. I recently sent a video of a new piece in my show to a friend. The guy's a genius. Within minutes he unlocked the issue that was holding back the piece. That realization may have taken me a year, maybe more. What a time saver. I'm really lucky to have access to people that can snap things into shape quickly. Having access to those friends is a blessing. Even if I didn't, that service can always be purchased, but I love working with friends.

I guess what I'm saying is this. If you want to get more corporate work, and ships, and theatres, etc… having the best website and promo and email CRM are nowhere near as important as having a killer show. If you have the best possible show and you keep improving it, I guarantee you'll get all the work, and all that stuff will follow. It's old advice, and when I started I didn't believe it. I also thought when I was in my 20's my act was as good as it could be. It wasn't. I look back after 30 years in the business. I realize that I'm not happy with the quality of the work I put out 10 years prior. You just don't know it at the time. Keep moving forward, I promise, none of us are as good as we think we are. Whip up the show to the best of your ability and everything else will fall in line.

There's todays thoughts on business from another idiot out in the trenches.

Until next time,
Good Night and Good Luck,
Jane Doe

Details of Art

It's all in the details.

Artistically I love to noodle around with details of my performance. Subconscious things the audience doesn't actually notice but can impact them. I've realized lately that my shows have been stronger because I've been finessing the staging and blocking. Most importantly, the PRE-SHOW staging and lighting.

It occurred to me (maybe finally) that what an audience sees when they enter the theatre to watch my show sets the tone. In a REALLY big way. What they see as they come in, and as they sit and get ready for things to start, makes a big difference. With graphics and lighting and music I've been able to create anticipation and a sense of fun without even having to walk onstage.

I perform often on cruises. I love the ships, food, people and shows. Their theatres are just amazing. It's by FAR my favourite theatres to perform in. That said I'd like the audience to really have the best time possible.

I've said this before and I'm repeating it. I know the demographic of this crowd, so I try to appeal to them. I have a graphic on screen and that graphic is in the style of Saul Bass, with lighting to complement. Saul is a personal favourite of mine when it comes to artists. If you're not familiar with him, Saul Bass did the title sequences of many movies from the 50's onward to the 90's. *Psycho*, *Anatomy of a Murder*, *Man with the Golden Arm*, *Vertigo*, *Casino* — you name it. His work is iconic. It's also timelessly cool. This graphic works because the older people in the audience see it and know what it is, a cool homage to Saul, and it instantly says what my show is about. It reminds them of those cool movies from the past, along with the pre-show music I play from those movie themes and puts them in a great mood. The younger people who don't know the films and Saul Bass's work see the image onscreen and think it's cool and funny. So, I win on both levels.

Young or old, the audience sees my stage set up and instantly knows there's something fun, magical and cool about to happen. No one has to say anything, they just absorb that information. While it's stylized, the picture of me tells them I wear a bowtie and that I don't take myself too seriously. It's exactly what I want for my audience to think before I begin to perform. It's a lot of win before they ever actually see me.

Something to be mindful of that can take a performance to another level. The more I pay attention to these things, the happier I am, the happier the audience is. It can't get better than that. The art is always in the details.

I'm also considering lighting my props with specials. Maybe not a bad idea. Maybe it is. We'll see.

See ya under the lighting grid.
Good Night and Good Luck,
Jane Doe

Writing

I make weird choices sometimes, especially when it comes to writing material. I have a strong belief that if I write what I like, the audience will sense that I'm doing something I love and get on board with that.

Doesn't always work, especially during the early days of a new hunk of material. This is happening right now. It's fun, and weird, and it's the job. Gotta suck it up.

If you've never created your own material or gone through the process of writing and then performing your own material, I can promise you this: It's HARD. So hard that you'll find yourself coming up with excuses not to do the new piece just to avoid having it see the stage and maybe have an audience not like it. Personally, I take the band aid approach to this: one rip... and boom, I jump right in. Even if the routine hasn't been completely written or the magic end of things blocked out the way I'd like, I go full Nike and just do it. I'm just strategic about the venues I do them.

A few weeks ago, I have a new piece in my show and I've been putting off birthing it onstage for the first time. Finally, I got so annoyed with myself that I decided enough is enough and put it in the show on a moment's notice. Second position in my performance in front of a thousand people. No real polish on the writing, NO blocking.... But there has to be a first time and you may as well do it when the stakes are high. Thousand people. Paying to see the best of you. If you're any kind of entertainer at all, you'll rise to the occasion. You'll come up with new lines. You'll come up with things on the spot and organize the piece appropriately. You'll also remember more doing it that way than if you'd rehearsed it a thousand times in your basement. I enjoy the thrill of maybe having something collapse early in your show and then have to dig your way out of the pit. So much a fan of the rush that I'm taping a TV show in two weeks and I'm doing a new piece on that TV show. Maybe been on stage four times with it. Stupid, you may say... but as papa Walenda says, "Life is on the wire, the rest is just waiting." There's a quote and theme that often recurs for me. No one ever looked back on their life and regretted the things they did do, only the stuff they didn't.

I write this to remind you to be brave and try new things. Doing material someone else wrote or created is boring and derivative and is something magicians do WAY too much. I have a friend out of L.A. who owns a pretty significant entertainment agency that books really high-end entertainment. Mostly comedians and magicians and speakers. We've been friends a long time and I've worked with his agency forever. He's my exclusive agent for cruise ships, and it's one of the best around, and he used to be a successful comedian. Let me tell you a quick story about this agent to illustrate why you should do different material.

I was staying at the agent's house in Los Angeles before doing a showcase for his buyers. As it often does while chatting in his backyard, the topic of magicians comes up. He said two things I think are striking and worth repeating. Not that I agree with him fully, but think about the perspective.

The first of his thoughts is that magicians would be better off if all magic shops closed. All of them. Too many acts buy the same crap and it dilutes not only the creative process but his ability to sell acts. The same tricks, the same lines. That's the REAL reputation of magicians around the world of booking agencies. It's the real answer to the question, "Why isn't there more magic on TV?" So, the closing of all shops might be harsh, but so be it, that's his opinion. The next thing I think is REALLY important. His criteria for booking magicians, be it comedy magician or straight magician, is this, again repeating the story: If you send him a promotional video and it has a rope routine, the production of a bowling ball, you make it snow, do the vanishing bandana or get out of a straitjacket, he dumps the tape and will not use you. I've seen him shut off a video seconds into it because a bowling ball was produced in the montage at the beginning of the tape.

At the time of writing in March of 2018, the effects listed above are omnipresent in magicians's shows. It's as if every act makes it snow and produces a bowling ball. It's getting out of hand. If you want to do a piece of magic you've seen another act do live or on television, just leave it alone and find or create something else. You'll be better for it in the long run. Have faith in yourself and you'll come up with cool stuff. Writing is the juice and it's why professional writers get paid so well. It all starts on the printed page.

You miss 100% of the shots you don't take.
Good night and good luck,
Jane Doe

Show Business or Show Art?

There's no star system in Canada. That's the problem.

I've been working in show business long enough that it's impossible not to be a little bit jaded by it. Since the age of 16, the showing of magic tricks and making them funny has been my sole source of income.

Starting out, it's everyone's wild ambition to be the next David Copperfield or George Carlin. Of course, the longer you keep at it, the less naïve you become. You realize there's a little more to it than that. I always thought magic specifically needed the equivalent of the A&R person in the music industry.

Someone to be the liaison between the artist and the agents, event planners, managers, and producers. Without that person, it's difficult to create good work, build an audience, AND do business and marketing. I believe, in part, the absence of an A&R person is what drove me in my teens to the world of conference performing. It seemed so impossibly impossible to become famous as a magician. I may as well go for the money and not waste my time trying to become a household name, that was the thinking of the day. This is Canada, there are no household names. Better to make bank, I thought, and have no one know my name than languish in poverty trying to build an audience that may never form. I probably should have gone after the audience. I may be happier now.

Every parent wants their kid to be the next Wayne Gretzky or Einstein. In my case I'd like my son Ferris to be the next Flaubert, Fran Lebowitz or even better, James Thurber (but with eyesight). The likelihood of achieving that level of quality is incredibly rare. REALLY rare. I think for his own comfort and security I'd rather him be like Stephen King or Clive Barker. Functional writers who make a lot of money. Their literature is neither crap nor ground breaking, but the general readership enjoys their work. And maybe their style, too. Certainly they are no Kurt Vonnegut or Philip Roth. I suppose that's what I am: the functional writer of live performance. I do very good, solid funny work, but I'm not breaking much new ground. I look back and think, what if I'd taken the chance to see what I could have built with the theatrical by going public? Instead, I chose to cater to the corporate conference and convention crowd. Had I chosen the former, I bet I'd have had something to say.

So there it is: What do you do? Run after the artistic goal of having an audience come to you? Do you develop an art that appeals to an existing audience? There's no support for new artists in Canada, little in the way of business help and the country is vast and wide. These things make touring difficult and expensive. Still, I think maybe I should have — but didn't. As a result, I am the conference and convention comedian and magician. Comedy Magic for Corporate Events — Take the Boredom out of the Boardroom. That's my slogan.

I may have made the right choice, but who knows.

I managed (so far) to beat the odds in the financial sense. I realize that the content of the work I've created does pander to the corporate environment and the people who attend its retreats and outings. I'm confident I can always go over very, very well at any corporate affair. If you'd asked the 17-year-old me if this is the material I'd dreamed of performing, I'd say that it's not. I'd rather be doing things that interest me. I once wanted to do a bullet catch routine whose story centred around William Burroughs shooting the apple off his wife's head. That seems infinitely more interesting than ripping up and restoring someone's Brooks Brothers suit jacket.

We all make our choices. I'm not really unhappy with mine. I have a very good life. Well, maybe a bit unhappy and riddled with doubts, but don't let me burden you with my troubles….

I wish Canada offered more support to young performing artists. Maybe I'd have taken greater risks and gone for something closer to what I truly wanted. No one can know for sure how it's going to turn out. I guess that's the problem and the lure of the arts. If you're truly an artist interested in creating satisfying work, there's a ton of risk involved, especially in my country. That's frightening, and who wants to end up broke.? Then again, as William H. Shedd says: "A ship is safe in harbour, but that is not what a ship is built for."

Something to think about, kids…. Hey, I see a ship in the harbour. It's Blue Monday, by New Order. Formerly Joy Division, formerly the Stiff Kittens.

Good Night and Good Luck,
Jane Doe

Discount Monkey

More than anything, stories and people like this are what drew me to show business.

I never met an act that hasn't at some point put money and time into a performance piece, only to find out it was a total waste of time. It's the way things are in the arts, I guess. That said, if you want to put money into something, think twice about an animal. Here's why.

We write bits together and for each other. That's how we roll. Fuelled by Mary Jane herself, my friend and I decided what his act needed is a live monkey playing the organ grinder throughout one of the pieces in his show. A throwback to old show business. Hard to train the animal to do it but worth the payoff, he said. This friend is one of those guys that'll take chances on something with long odds of paying off, just to maybe bump up his show. It's a quality I've always admired.

In the late 80's / early 90's, getting a monkey at a pet store here in Toronto was pretty easy. Exotic animals were everywhere, unlike now, when they can only be seen at zoos and magic shows in Niagara Falls with a two-drink minimum.

It's quite a thing to walk into a store and see not only a monkey for sale, but one marked down from 250 dollars, to 150, to 100, to 75 dollars. Discount Monkey. Brilliant. Even I know bargain-basement price slashing does not instill a sense of quality in pet purchases. The fact that the monkey was grabbing the bars, shaking and screaming like it was trying to get out of Shawshank didn't sit well with me. My guess is that it was angry and someone had given it booze. Still, my friend thought this was the perfect monkey, not because it was a good, trainable pet, but because it was priced right. It was 175 dollars cheaper than any other monkey, and who doesn't love a bargain? Protesting that monkeys are a "get-what-you-pay-for" kind of pet, and a cursory evaluation of its demeanour suggesting that this may not be the most trainable monkey that "family audiences would love and adore," I suggested that it may be useless for our purposes, but he didn't listen. In the end, the monkey was bought. Long odds indeed.

The monkey wore a blue jumpsuit, like the one Hannibal wore in *Silence of the Lambs,* so we called him Dr. Lecter. Once in the car, Lecter began to live up to his name. Hannibal was screaming, ripping his wee jump suit and throwing a total fit. My friend suggested that all he needed was a banana and some love. Yeah, and maybe 300 CC's of thorazine. Twenty-five minutes in the passenger seat with a screaming monkey hissing and spitting from a cage on your lap tests the limits of friendship. But he'd helped me steal a camel on an overseas tour, so I owed him. What's a guy to do?

Once home, it took all of 5 minutes to destroy the apartment. It pulled the phone cord out of the wall, shredded curtains, ripped up books and movies and expelled waste in no less than 4 parts of the house. It was literally loosing its shit.

In hindsight, we never should have taken its jumpsuit off. Clearly it was a prison monkey: institutionalized and unable to function on "The Outside." Left to its own devices, it would have written, "Brooks was here" on the wall.

Two hours of chasing the devil's spawn around the apartment led to more destruction and its final capture. We cornered it with two juggling clubs and a Morrisey Coin Pail. Turns out their hand-spun metal products really are very tough. I recommend it for "the worker."

This was not the loveable monkey who would sit on his shoulder and play music while my friend did magic. At best it might rip his ear off and string it on a chain around its neck, while going upriver on a raft to ask Colonel Kurtz why we lost the war in Viet Nam. It finally dawned on us that perhaps Doctor Lecter needed to be sent back to the prison. Senator, … love your suit.

It was a monster. We knew it and so did the pet shop. It turns out when a pet shop sells a mentally unstable animal they instantly develop a "no refund policy." The spawny bastards.

Getting rid of the monkey was now the priority. We made up posters and put them around the east end of the city. From the street we could still hear the monkey screaming and rattling its cage. Luckily it didn't take more than an hour for the phone to ring. Some poor unsuspecting soul wanted the monkey and it was agreed he would pay 50 bucks for it. 49.99 too much.

At the appointed time, 50-dollar guy shows up, pays and picks up the beast. Naturally the monkey was screaming like it has PTSD after several tours of duty with the marines. To his credit, my friend told the buyer that the animal needed to be fed and that explained his disgruntled attitude. Since the purchaser had parked his car in front of the apartment on the street, we didn't even need to help him out to the car. The ordeal was over. He would take Dr. Lecter home and we'd be free to carry on with a trip to the Court Jester bar.

Doors locked and lights turned off, we peeked through what was left of the curtains and watched him get the monkey into the car. Once in, the fool unleashed the monkey and all of Hell by opening the cage door. I can't believe he did that. If you've seen *Jurassic Park* when Wayne Knight is attacked in his Jeep by the small dinosaur, that's pretty much what we witnessed.

It took 30 minutes to get Dr. Lecter back in the cage. 30 minutes of us laughing… then it happened. Out of the car he and the cage started back toward the building.

We had to be quiet. The door was locked but we still didn't feel safe. The buyer of devil monkey was screaming and kicking the door. Yelling at us to take "this f#$CKING monkey back." People on the street began to gawk. He kicked at the door for about 20 minutes, yelling things like "I know you're in there" and "You screwed me over, I'll kick your ass."

> *Pro tip: This has been a theme for my friend and I. On the road, we've run into this door-kicking scenario 15 times at least. I think our off-stage antics encourage it. I'm not sure. Be careful when you tour with us.*

Back to the apartment. We stayed put, quiet… drinking beer, letting all this play out. The guy screaming, combined with a bit of drunken buzz, we started to giggle, which turned into a laugh. The guy could hear us now.

With one last thunderous bang on the door the guy yells "I know you're in there, I can hear you asses laughing. Take this godless monkey back!!" (EXACT quote)

It might have been the beer or just plain exhaustion but finally my friend, beer in hand yelled back "there's no one home!" This prompted a last scream of "How F**King stupid are you?" For lots of reasons, the answer to that is… VERY.

A few more expletives from the monkey buyer and he gave up. We watched him take the primate back to his car and drive away. I always wondered what happened to poor little Doctor Lectre. The writer Hunter S. Thompson sums it up best in *Fear and Loathing in Las Vegas*, unknowingly giving the perfect description of that animal:

"There he goes. One of God's own prototypes. A high-powered mutant of some kind never even considered for mass production. Too weird to live, and too rare to die."

The moral here is this. Learn a side steal. A double lift. Write your act. Work the stage, buy Morrisey, And if you're gonna get a monkey, don't buy discount.

Thoughts from the road zoo.
Good night and good luck,
Jane Doe

Etiquette of the Comedy Club

Lesson in showbiz. Mid to late 90's, I'm working a theatre in Belleville with four other act friends. Magician, juggler, mime, that kinda line up. Telemarketing show. All solid acts. The closing act is going on WAY too long, likely day drunk. Because I'm his regular drinking buddy, producer says I have to be the one to pull him off stage (or maybe because I'm the youngest on the bill). I run into his dressing room and get his trench coat, walk out onstage where he's doing some bit and like they did with James Brown and the cape, I put the jacket over him and I sing: "Please… please… please… can we go home." Audience amazingly gets the reference and laughs. I think I've capped the show and it's done. The act drops his props and walks offstage with me, audience applauding. Just like James Brown, I've got my arm around him, and halfway across the stage, he stops, throws the jacket off and yells "NO ! I can do more!", then runs back to centre stage to juggle some stuff. Audience explodes. He walks off, just destroying the room. THAT… is showbiz.

Comedy club owner in Canada was legendarily nice about giving younger acts their first headline job. Myself included, I was about 23. My first night in, there's 2 guest spots. First up is Rick Overton (The Drake on *Seinfeld*). He blows the lid off the room, I'm backstage, thinking how bad this is, bad for me, no way I can follow this. Then I look at the sheet and the next guest spot before I go out is David Acer. Phew, I think, I can follow another magician, this is gonna be ok. Sweet damn, he just KILLED — it's hard to describe how much he killed. No magic, just purely awesome stand-up. I'm backstage, thinking, "It shouldn't be this way the first time…." I went out and died. I died right in front of Brent Schiess, booker for *Just for Laughs* who thought he'd come see the new young turk. When the universe kicks you in the balls, it kicks hard.

Depressed, I go back up to the condo. The phone rings, a woman asks for the owner of the club. Sorry, I say, he's not here, he's at home. She asks for his home number… and I GAVE IT TO HER !!! OMG, what an idiot I am. Next day, club owner is screaming at me that his wife is pissed off, she knows about this other woman and she outed him. Turns out the comedy condo was also the owners sex pad on the side. I'm early 20's… what did I know. Point is, he was pissed off, so pissed off I never worked the club again. EVER.

Point of the story is: 1) never underestimate any act, ever and 2) never give out a phone number of someone you're working for. And 3) Dave Acer is a monster stand-up... wow... just wow.

Good night and good luck,
Jane Doe

My Questionable Fame in the Gay Community

While I'm not gay, I've been blessed to be looked after by that crowd. I was always lucky to fall in with a crowd of artistic, gay, cool people. When my ex split, I was left financially and emotionally bankrupt. Gay community to the rescue. Not sure I'd have survived that without their support. First night we go to Zippers in Toronto. Gat dance club… 80's night but the gay community doesn't mind my dancing like a straight white man. I'd have understood if they did. It's easily the most inclusive community ever, but there's snickers at my lame and hammered dancing, I know it.

Prior to that we go to a smaller club in the gaybourhood. It's filled with about 300 people, where there's a drag show in progress. The headliner of that drag show recognizes me from TV. From the stage she announces "Wow, it's Matt from TV, come up here !!" I don't want to go, I know where this leads. I drunkenly and reluctantly walk up to the stage. Into the mic she says, "You're so funny, I saw you on TV doing magic. Hey everyone… applaud if you saw Matt on TV!"

That is when 300 people remained completely silent. Not a fucking soul made a peep or knew who I was, because, I'm not anyone.

"Oh," she says, trying to walk it back… "Well then… let's get back to the show," and sends me back to the dance floor.

That one hurt.

Welcome to Canada where, as Foster says, "You can die of exposure."

Upside of the story is, I ended up making out with one of the straight girls who was the straight wife of one of the gay girls. Somehow that felt like a victory. Point is, comedian, magician, anything on Canadian TV means zilch, but ALWAYS the gay community has your back. I am, and always will be, forever in debt to your timeless saving of my mental health… my liver may also thank you… maybe.

Keep on dancin'.
Good Night and Good Luck,
Jane Doe

Radio Personality

It's Frenchie Craig McFarlane's birthday. Q107's Jacques Le-Strap. He was doing comedy in Toronto BEFORE there were comedy clubs. At a gig in Ottawa mid 90's, during a particularly difficult time to obtain hash or any drug, really, Frenchie assures me he's got "a guy" for after the show. He'll hook us up but we gotta talk in code, because these new cell phones aren't safe.

1am back at the hotel. Frenchie calls his guy. In his French accent says, "We're at X hotel, come over… it's h-ash Wednesday." Dealer, super high himself, replies, "What?" Frenchie again says, "It's haaaaaash Wednesday." "What??" says the dealer. Frenchie again, "It's hAAsh Wednesday," trying to emphasize it any way he can. I hear the dealer through the phone say, "What are you talkin' about, man?" Then, uncharacteristic of Frenchie, he snaps and yells, "Just bring the fuckin' hash !!!" and slams the phone.

So many great stories with you, sir, and thanks for booking me in my teens when I probably didn't deserve it, and for throwing me some 175 dollar gig when I REALLY needed the money to make ends meet.

All that is one of the many reasons I love the business. Smoke 'em if ya got 'em.

Good Night and Good Luck,
Jane Doe

Online Booking Sites

Sure, you may get gigs from these things, and I get that everyone needs money. Disclosure: I love doing absurd quotes on those sites (it's my new hobby). 5 bucks, 500, 5000, 200. What's interesting is I never get the gigs, no matter how much I experiment and dick around, because there's always someone cheaper. This is the arts. You're not buying underwear. You don't want to be in the position to be undercut. They have to want to buy YOU.

Look, I'm not telling you what to do, but may I suggest that you don't want to work for people who are only concerned with the price of your work. 30 years in this business tells me they're always a pain in the ass. They don't value your years of work, experience, and talent. If they're about price only, I PROMISE you they don't care about working with you on the correct performing conditions and everything else to make sure you're successful. They don't. You're an afterthought. They're often spending more on giveaways at that point.

Y'know, if you're 500 bucks or even a thousand or 1500 at some corporate thing, they're spending more on food and decor than they are on you. You're supposed to be the highlight of the evening. If they spend less on you than they do on ancillary things, you think they're gonna haul ass to make sure there's no dance floor ahead of you? Or the sound system is appropriate? Or lighting? Or follow a rider?? Hell, no. Then, when the performance doesn't go well, it's easy to gripe and blame everything on you. No audience in the history of ever saw a bad performer at an event and thought, "I bet that dude's show was crap because, wow, the sound and lights are terrible, and look how far away we are from him." It doesn't happen. They just watch and say the act is terrible. That's the memory.

As young kid, not but 15, it was old man Craig Frenchie McFarlane told me, "No cover, no respect. Everyone throws a 500 dollar act under the bus but no one does that with a 5 or 10 thousand dollar act." You know what, he was right. You gotta know what your talent is worth, don't give it away to shit conditions and to buyers that don't care. Don't do it. Your efforts are worth more than that. YOU are worth more than that.

That said, I once performed in a bath house.... But that was for the story, not the money (I am who I am, I can't help it). You know what I mean.

Just a thought.
Good Night and Good Luck,
Jane Doe

Thinkin' Out Loud

For the acts, the magicians and all the talent. Everyone says they're an artist but there's no real test of it. I wonder. Say a billionaire came along and said, "I'll float you, your whole life, everything, but you gotta take your work somewhere different and original, I want to see things no one's seen before." … I mean, could you do it? I don't think I can, but maaaybe I can. Do you have any ideas right now worth working on, unmarketable plots but something's there… maybe reworking things never seen before of 100 years past? Some crazy idea you've had but you were afraid to put it on stage because you've gotta make money and by default, be commercial enough to be marketable enough so you pay the mortgage.

But, say that didn't come into play, say you could be like Eric Bogosian and that Joe Papp says the public theatre is yours… have at it, create something. Imagine if that was the mindset from the very beginning when we started. Be interesting, right? Wonder what you'd come up with. Again, I'm just thinkin' out loud… who needs the billionaire. Put the work out there and see where it goes. Magic especially has a TON of overlap you don't see in other performing arts. Maybe time to ditch it. Change the culture.

It's getting harder and harder to be a full-time act anyway, so why not try something new and stupid and crazy and different? You're an artist, supposed to go broke anyway.

Variety artists especially are guilty of being architects of their own demise. Agents often say there's a host of material that's overdone but very commercial. It's not artistically satisfying, but the crowds like it. What's the win in that? I'm guilty of it myself, though I push against it….

Just saying….

If you're lucky you'll be allowed the freedom to fail. A cruise director (I love you, Jairo Lobo) saw me do this new piece that just sucked. Weekly it sucked. It didn't get laughs, sometimes it also didn't mechanically work. Fly out and back in a week later, and the piece continued to suck. Rinse repeat, week after week. Every time I flew back in, the piece sucked. But it got better in small bits each time. He never ratted me out to the booker because I asked him to give me 6 months and he'd see the piece sing. It did, but he let me bone that routine and kept quiet about it so I kept my job. WE NEED MORE OF THAT TOO!

Take a risk, what the hell….
Good Night and Good Luck,
Jane Doe

Scouted

Some important magician or agent or buyer in the house.... First reaction is you're afraid to suck... don't want the other pros see you eat it, so you dump to crowd-pleasing stuff. We all gotta nut up and eat it for a while, and hope Karma carries our career.

Quick story, my fist time headlining at a comedy club in Montreal, it just happened the booker for *Just for Laughs* was in that night to see someone do a spot and stuck around for my set. Worthy of note: he DID stay and watched my show (shocking). For my original material off the top of the set, he stayed, but the minute I went into a stock, time-filler piece, he bolted right outta that audience, never to be heard from again (fuck you Brent, I'd have bought you drinks that night). Point is, ain't never gonna level up with stock material or being a fax of someone else. We can all learn from that. Never going anywhere with anything they can see someone else do better... so what's the point? Already one Mac King, right? (I've still never seen him live, I gotta get around to that.)

Imagine if the variety community embraced the suck and built on it, like comics do... where might we be?

Mid-day ramblings, I'm not attacking anyone, I'm just saying I'm not sure we're helping ourselves by being another Don Allen or Dave Williamson or Copperfield.

Magicians really need to give themselves the freedom to suck, imagine that.

Pass the bong,
Good Night and Good Luck,
Jane Doe

Charity Events

Three-hundred person black tie event at the Ritz-Carlton, Toronto. Fundraiser. Full sit-down dinner. Will I headline the event for free for a tax receipt?, the organizer asks by email.

Umm, if it came with a blowjob from Drew Barrymore, I'd still tell them to take a giant leap into Lake Go Fuck Yourself.

What's that, a thousand bucks a plate? Is the hotel donating for free? The catering company? The A/V company donating their services? No, they aren't.... What right do you have to ask ME to work for free AND BE THE HIGHLIGHT OF THE NIGHT!?

Worst of all, they'll find some act who'll do it. It's the amateurs that make it hard for the professionals to survive.

Not to sound like Harlan Ellison here, but pay the writer. I agree with him 100%.

Damn. Sorry for the rant. Bitter but still happy.

Good Night and Good Luck,
Jane Doe

Sketchy Producer Lessons from the Past, Submitted for your Approval

A bus ticket from Korea. For the lessons it reminds me of, I'll never get rid of it. In 1997 I did my first tour overseas. I'd performed in the USA and Canada and the UK, but not on the other side of the world, where language was an issue. Producer hires me, but it's a last minute booking, so he says I have to buy the airfare, then get reimbursed. Toronto > Vancouver > Anchorage > Seoul, that's the route, Korean Air. Someone will meet me at the airport, says the booker, they'll take me to Taejon. I'll live at the hotel for the duration of the run and the theatre is right next door. Another Canadian act performs onsite; he'll help me with language, etc.

I arrive in Seoul, no one meets me. I wait. Hours later, dude looking like Oddjob from the Bond films shows up, sign in hand with my name on it. He takes me to a bus station 20 minutes away from the airport, turns to me and says, "Take bus to Taejon." He gets out, drops my bags at the curb and drives away. Korean-to-English dictionary and some American cash gets me by enough to purchase a bus ticket and something to drink. Hours of work to accomplish that. Finally get to the gig in town. It's not a theatre, it's a theme park. I'm living ON a fucking theme park (Kumdori Land) in the non-air conditioned apartments above the offices. The Canadian act left me after my first 45 minutes off the bus. He was going home and gave me a sheet of Korean phrases I could use, then he got on a bus and split. He knew when it was time to get out.

There was no theatre. Just an outdoor stage, middle of the park. A stage in August 80 degree heat (Nielsen palming coins in that heat lead to the image of Norm being burned into your palm like that guy in Indiana Jones with the hot medallion). Every morning woken up by screams of children from the looping pirate ship. For three weeks I opened for Russian dancers in the blazing hot sun, on a metal stage, 4 shows a day wearing a suit, because that's all I had to wear after being promised I'd be performing in an air conditioned theatre.

The game became this: Time the magic so the screams and applause from the bungee jump ride next to the stage made it sound like it was for me. After each show I'd go back to the room, strip off the suit, let it hang to dry and lie on the bed with a fan pointed at my junk. (That failed to cool, just so you know.)

I never got paid for the flights or gig, the producer stole the money. I'd also left the contract several days early because North Korea was threatening to invade (I had no idea this was common) and, freaking out, I'd bribed a ride operator with a marginal grasp of English to drive me back to Seoul and the airport in the middle of the night. He played Metallica's "King Nothing" on repeat for the whole 2 hours. You haven't lived until you've heard James Hetfield sing the same song for 2 hours, and after that you don't want to live.

Point is this: I wouldn't change any of it. Not one thing. It taught me how to deal with producers and the road. Contracts, payment and travel. You need to get burned early in your career. I had this and a cruise ship for education early on. Best way to learn. No school or book or online class can teach what you learn by doing. I didn't get paid in cash, but what I learned about the business was priceless. I try to tell younger acts that in the end, never pass up an opportunity to gig anywhere, you don't know where it will lead. In my case it lead to Norm burnt into my hands, sleeping with Russian dancers, street drinking and to always get a healthy deposit.

Good Night and Good Luck,
Jane Doe

Special Thanks

If you got this far, I can't believe it. Thank you. I owe a debt of gratitude to all my showbiz and artist friends who've helped my career along the way. Advice, stories, helping me level up, all that sort of thing. No career without them, so a special thanks to the good ones, in no particular order.

Glenn Ottaway, Wes Zaharuk, David Ben, David Peck, the Evasons, David Merry, Steve Smith, Ron Reid, Martin Lewis, Russell Peters, Micheal Ross, Mike Bullard, Tony Molesworth, Winston Spear, Jay Sankey, Gary Kurtz, Ed Smeall, Richard Sanders, Willis Kenny, Tom Stade, Stewart Francis, and ten thousand other acts and agents I've met and worked with along the way. Each one did something for me. I'd never have got here alone, that's for sure.

About the author

Matthew DiSero starred on the most exclusive television show for magicians — *Penn and Teller: Fool Us* and headlines at the world-famous Magic Castle in Hollywood, California. As a comedian and magician, he has been nominated for a Canadian Comedy Award and invited to perform at Canada's Walk of Fame Ceremonies. Appearances at The Great Lakes Comedy Festival in Cleveland, Moncton's Hubcap comedy festival, and the Edmonton and Regina Comedy Festivals have made Matt a sought after and in demand public and corporate entertainer.

With television appearances on the Comedy Network, Comedy Central, CBC, The CW network and even Netflix; he can also be heard on XM radio and podcasts across the globe. Truly an international artist, Matt also takes the stage headlining his favourite luxury cruise lines Royal Caribbean, Princess and Holland America Line. Touring his show to exotic locales such as Tokyo, Italy, South America and Australia, Matthew also donates his comedic talents to both the Canadian and American Militaries for morale boosting shows to raise the spirits of troops in Kuwait, Korea, Afghanistan, Bosnia and even the North Pole. Matt is no fan of Podium.

Made in United States
Troutdale, OR
06/07/2023

10488349R00063